VIOLENCE AND TERROR
SIAMESE TWINS

VIOLENCE AND TERROR

Siamese Twins

Joseph Benjamin

GYAN

ISBN: 978-81-212-1228-1

Price: ₹ 550

First Published, 2014

Published by

Gyan Publishing House
23, Main Ansari Road
Daryaganj, New Delhi-110002
Phones: 23282060, 23261060
Fax : 91-11-23285914
E-mail: books@gyanbooks.com

Laser Typesetting: Gyan Print (AB-I)

Printed at: Chawla Offset Printers, Delhi

Cataloging in Publication Data—DK

Courtesy: D.K. Agencies (P) Ltd. <docinfo@dkagencies.com>

Violence and terror : siamese twins / Joseph Benjamin.
p. cm.
Contributed articles.
Includes bibliographical references and index.
ISBN 9788121212281

1. Violence—India. 2. Terrorism—India. I. Benjamin, Joseph, Dr.

DDC 303.60954 23

Contents

Preface

Violence is the innate instinct of all living creatures, whether animal or human being. The utilisation of physical force or power as a means of achieving ends is called as violence. All creatures are easily moved to anger and fight in attack or self-defence. Actually, the history of man is a history of perpetual conflict. Violence is a complex problem, arising out of psychological, cultural, political and religious factors. By very nature, violence is a destructive force; and, hence, needs to be curbed. The problem of violence is of almost importance today. No one escape the realisation that we are living through one of the greatest crisis of civilisation characterised by increasing violence and terror. In our fragmented social structure violence has employed as a dominant mode of social interaction and this mode is mostly influenced by politics.

On the other hand terror is feeling of extreme fear. It is a situation or thing that makes one very afraid. Sometime violent action or the threat of violent action is intended to cause fear. Violence and terror are destructive. It causes damage to individual and property. Hence, both have to be curbed. Similarly, terrorism is the use of violence action in order to achieve political aims or force a government to act. Terrorists attack the innocent people including children and women and create violence in the state for political motives. Both violence and terror are to be taken as Siamese Twins. Both create cerotic situation in our society.

This book is the collection of research papers written by various experts from varied disciplines and professions. Attempt is made to study violence and terror in different forms.

I have been supported by my family members; my wife Smt. Pratibha, my sons namely, Prashant and Jayant who have shown patience during my work.

Joseph Benjamin

Introduction

Joseph Benjamin

According to the Random House Dictionary of English Language, "Violence means rough or injurious physical force, action or treatment". In other words, it is the expression of an individual's aggressive drive on both the personal and social levels. Personal violence is a violent act of a man or woman against another man or woman—such as assault and rape, homicide. Social violence, on the other hand, is manifested in actions and situations like genocide, the concentration camps set up by the Nazi regime in Germany to exterminate Jews during the Second World War and communal riots. Some scholars have tried to relate violence with aggression. However, Daniels has a different view in this regard. He points out that 'aggression' represents an entire spectrum of assertive, intrusive and attacking behaviour. Violence, as a specialised sub-form of aggression, is accompanied by a strong, uncontrollable emotion like anger or hostility; and anger occurs when a plan of action towards a valued goal is interrupted by something specific enough to warrant attack (Daniels, D.N., 1970: 98) or "when the expected rewards for attack override other outcomes" (*ibid.*, 14). According to the Encyclopedia of Social Sciences, (Sidney, 1935: 264) in the social context, violence may be roughly defined as the illegal employment of methods of physical coercion for achieving personal or group ends. It is distinct from force or power, which is a purely physical concept. The use of physical force or brute power for achieving one's ends is called violence. Violence connotes force. Webster's Collegiate Dictionary (10th edition) describes violence as the 'exertion of physical force as far as to injure or abuse.'

It is an innate instinct witnessed in all living creatures, be they human or animal. Violence may be the consequence of anger or an individual's reaction of self-defence in what s/he perceives to be a threatening situation. Human history is replete with instances of perpetual conflict that are manifested in violence. The human being is the source and object of violence. Violence is actually a complex problem, arising out of various psychological, cultural, political and religious factors. By its very nature, it is a destructive force and needs to be curbed at the very outset. The problem of violence has assumed alarming proportions in the contemporary era, which is characterised by rapidly escalating violence and terror, which have infested virtually all sections of society and impacted virtually every nation in the world.

The use of force is an intrinsic act of violence, be it physical or psychological. Coercion is the use of either physical or intangible force to compel action that is contrary to the will or reasoned judgment of the individual or group subjected to such force. The violence is the willful application of a force in way that it physically or psychologically injures or causes damage to the person, group or property against whom it is applied.

The term 'violence' is also associated with several meanings, as can be observed in the rapidly growing literature on the subject. The dictionary meaning of 'violence' is the exercise of physical force so as to inflict injury or damage to any person(s) or property. This infliction of injury or damage could be both spiritual and non-spiritual. In both the senses, however, violence leads to destructiveness, and symbolises an act perpetrated by one person against the freedom of another.

Newton Graver (Newton Graver, 1970: 349-370) has identified four manifestations of violence:

(a) Personal overt physical assault, where one inflicts physical harm to another.

(b) When physical assault is practiced in corporate terms, it becomes institutionalised overt physical assault. A clear example is war, where someone for example, a society, a state, a group) mobilises its resources specifically for corporate acts of killing and destruction. For example Gujarat riot 2002 and Khandamal violence 2009.

(c) Personal covert violence, when an individual violates the personhood of another in ways that are psychologically destructive, rather than inflicting physical harm.

(d) Institutionalised covert violence, this happens when the structures of society or institutions violates the personhood of members of a society. Caste system, practice of untouchability and pollution-purity practice are clear examples of such violence. 'Children of lesser gods' experience such violence all the time.

The violence has started just from the creation of mankind. The violence can be traced back to the times of Abel and Cain, as mentioned in the Old Testament Bible of the Christians and Jews. As has been mentioned above, violence can be considered as a form of unsanctioned damage to any person or property. In ancient societies, man would glory in the use of violence and the man of war would be considered a hero. It is no wonder then that violence also has a scriptural sanction. Since scriptures are ancient books of authority, many primordial instincts and customs find a justification in some of these sacred books. Even today, the practice of sacrificing children to god for some wish fulfilment in return is prevalent in Indian society. There are also instances of human beings having been sacrificed to please the god of rain and engender bountiful rainfall in return (Gupta, 1945: 194). The history of the world thus shows that violence is a universal phenomenon. Even more paradoxical is the close relationship between violence and human progress as has been seen through the side effects of war. Ironically, advancements in science and technology have not been able to achieve any reduction in violence but have, in fact, provided more effective and more reliable instruments of perpetrating torture and violence on humans. Developments in science are indeed directly proportional to developments in various forms of violence. Today we have the nuclear bomb, which is a potential threat to all of humanity in the entire universe. More and more weapons continue to be manufactured to unleash waves of violence and to destroy humanity in all corners of the globe (Aiyar, 1967: 29-30). Manufacturing nuclear bomb is not to be considered as sign for development of any country, because it would cause violence and lead to the destruction of world. Violence causes unsanctioned damage to person and property. The difference between violence and terrorism is very subtle. Both lead damage to individual and property.

Terrorism means compelling someone or terrifying someone to act according to one's own wish. Whenever one talks of terrorism, immediately one asks oneself where terrorism exists. Whenever one thinks of terrorism, America, Afghanistan, some part of South Asia, Kashmir and Punjab comes to one's mind. One feels that terrorism exists only in these places. Terrorism exists everywhere in the world. Terrorism means terrifying or threatening someone. Sometime teachers create fear in the minds of students in order to correct them. The way mother-in-law treats her daughter-in-law in a terrified manner can be considered as a form of terrorism. Terrorism exists in every society and each branch of our life. Terrorism exists everywhere, in a family, society, nations and in the world. Terrorism has been defined by many scholars differently. It is difficult to speak about terrorism without discussing the historical context of the terrorist campaign. Modern terrorism originated from French revolution (1789-1795). It was used as a term to describe the actions of the French government. By 1848, the meaning of terrorism changed. It was employed to describe violent revolutionaries who revolted against governments. By the end of the 1800s and early 1900s, terrorism was used to describe the violent activities of a number of groups including: labour organisations, anarchists, nationalist groups revolting against foreign powers and ultranationalist political organisations.

After World War II (1939-1945), the meaning of terrorism again changed. As people revolted from European domination of the world, nationalistic groups were deemed to be terrorist groups. Again from 1964 to early 1980s, the term terrorism was also applied to violent left-wing groups, as well as nationalists. In the mid-1980s, the meaning changed again. In United States, some of the violent activities of the hate movement were defined as terrorism. Internationally, terrorism was viewed as sub-national warfare. Recently a Sikh professor Prabhjot Singh at Columbia University was attacked and injured by a mob of up to 30 people who called him "Osama" and "terrorist" during a brutal assault, which the police is investigating as hate crime (Indian Express, September 24, 2013, p. 2).

As the millennium changed, the definition of terrorism also changed. Today, terrorism also refers to large groups who consider themselves as independent from state, violent religious fanatics, and violent groups who terrorise for a particular cause or demand. Today the terrorists may not be having demand but only to terrorise the innocent people. It may be to have fame in the world or capture power. Whatever may be definition, terrorism leads to violence and injure individuals. Violence and terrorism go together. One cannot see terrorism without violence.

The present book is the collection of papers on violence and terror. Scholars from different fields were asked to send paper on terror and violence. These papers on violence and terror were sent by experts on request.

Leela D'Souza in her paper "Communal Violence in India: A Crisis of Identity" has said that today communal violence has taken different expressions, not just between religious communities. It includes ethnic (including tribal), caste, regional and language communities like the demands in Punjab for a separate Khalistan, the struggles in north-east India between tribal communities and non-tribal, the claims of the Shiv Sena and the Maharashtra Navnirman Sena in Maharashtra, which are cases of communal violence. She says that the increasing incidences of communal violence in recent times can be closely linked to the crisis of identity.

Manoj Kumar Jha in his paper "Living Together Separately" states that the episodes of violence between religious communities have generally been explained as symptomatic of a society which has 'forgotten' the skills of plural living and togetherness. In his paper an attempt is made to place the riots in the larger context of rapidly changing nature of the spaces in which human beings chose to interact or remain oblivious of each other. His paper also aims at placing the larger frames of violence and the violent structures besides the smaller frame of gradual but systematic reduction in the size of the moral community. An attempt is also made to problematise the simplistic interpretation of any act of violence as occurring between persons identified as belonging to different religious groups.

Joseph Benjamin in his paper, "Violence against Christian" has tried to study communal violence of 2009 in Odisha. Before studying the violence against Christians, he has tried to define violence. He tries to explain how the Adivasis in Odisha, who have embraced Christianity, are being attacked by other religious fundamentalists. The anti-Christian violence has been having serious sociological repercussion in small town and villages, especially the places where Adivasis concentration is more.

Oinam Jitendra Singh in paper "Impunity, Fake Encounter and Human Rights in Manipur" study the presence of security forces in Manipur. The phenomenon of indiscriminate and arbitrary killing by the security forces on the local population continues throughout the years. The Arbitrary killing in the pretext of counter insurgency is not only justified but consider as necessary pattern to tackle the law and order situation in Manipur. In this present paper he tries to analyse the practice of extrajudicial or extralegal killing in Manipur by the State security forces within the human rights framework, which the government of India has obligation. It is well aware that both the state and non-state actors perpetrate serious form of Human Rights violation by giving their own justification.

S. Mangi Singh in his paper "Challenges to Free and Fair Elections in the Hills of Manipur: A Study of the ADC Elections 2010" has tried to study the Manipur Election in 2010. He says that Free and fair elections are one of the most essential pre-requisites for any democratic political system. It facilitates meaningful representation of the people in matters of governance, and lends credence to freedom of political expression, freedom of speech, freedom of choice, etc., which are available to the people of a country. The subject matter of his paper is being located in the context of considerations with the hypothesis that free and fair election is becoming more of a myth than a reality in the *Naga* dominated areas of the hills of Manipur.

Gladson Dungdung in his paper "Understanding Adivasis Violence" says that human rights of the Adivasis are being violated. The matter for the biggest concern is that today large number of *Adivasi* youth have taken up the guns after being influenced by some ultra-left groups. He tries to examine why a peace-loving community has adopted the path of violence. Why do youth see the gun as panacea for their problems? Why did the Indian State fail to contain the discontents? What went wrong with the Indian democracy after 67 years of Independence which put the community on the path of Violence? Why have the guns become a part of life for the villagers in the mineral-rich corridor? He made an attempt to find out the answers to these questions in his paper.

Mohan Kashikar in his paper "Terrorism: Anatomy and Prevention" says that terrorism has become a global menace today and has attracted the attention of the entire world after September 11, 2001. India is the country which has suffered the most due to this menace. This greatest challenge to the humanity in the 21st century had its roots in the 20th century. In his paper he made an attempt to understand the definition, characteristics and development of 'Terrorism'; India's case and her response to it; its global face and possible solutions to tackle this menace.

Kartik Lokhande in his paper "Naxalism and Violence" has tried to study the genesis and causes of Naxalism. He said that Naxalism, in its original form, was a reaction by the oppressed and exploited masses to get justice with the help of arms, it received support from the intelligentsia in several parts of the country. He wants to make a few suggestions and urges the Government as well as various constituents of the society to think over the problem killing of innocents and come up with refinements with an aim to achieve the peaceful coexistence of all sections.

Ram Puniyani in his paper "Politics of Terror and Contemporary Times" says that the current times are full of insane acts of terror. All over the globe and also in India acts of violence by political groups seeking justice or revenge are dime a dozen. September 11, 2001 brought to fore this dreaded phenomenon and global attention has been glued to this phenomenon. In this attack over three thousand innocent people died. Later many a terror attacks were witnessed in Pakistan, Afghanistan and other places. Not a month passes when one does not hear about the death of innocents in one more such act in one or the other corner of the globe. India has been tragically witnessing these acts of terror. He makes a survey of number of riots which took place in India.

Asghar Ali Engineer in his paper "Communal Riots 2011" has made a study of communal riots took place from January to

December 2011. He said that during 2011, the communal riots took place on extremely petty issues. He also adds that poverty and unemployment makes it possible for large number of people to gather and take part in rioting.

I thank each and every scholar who has helped enormously in the preparation of this volume. I requested these scholars to send paper on a very pertinent issue. The contributors are from different fields and also expert in their own areas. I would further submit that these research papers are original and of high quality of scholarship.

I will be happy to have comments and feedback on this path breaking book entitled, Violence and Terror: Siamese Twins, which is becoming a turbulent and intractable issue in the arena of political discourse in our Indian Politics.

References

Daniels, D.N., et al., (1970): Violence and the Struggle for Existence, Little Brown and Company, Boston.

Gupta, Narendra Nath (1945). "Side Lights on the National Movement in India", Vol. I, *Gandhi and Gandhism*, Kitabs, Bombay, p. 194.

Hook, Sidney (ed.) (1935). Violence, *In Encyclopaedia of the Social Sciences*, Vol. 15, Macmillan Company, New York.

Aiyar, S.P. (1967). "Anatomy of Mass Violence", in S.P. Aiyar (ed.) *The Politics of Mass Violence in India*, Manaktala and Sons, Bombay, pp. 29-30.

Newton Graver, 1970 "What Violence is" in Philosophy for a New Generation A.K. Bierman and James Gould, ed. New York: Macmillan, pp. 349-370, as given by Joel E. Tabora, "On Violence, Force and Rational Necessity," in *Pulso*, Vol. I. No. 2. 1985, p. 100.

List of Contributors

Joseph Benjamin, Currently he is Associate Professor and Head, Department of Political Science, St. Francis De Sales College, Nagpur. He is conferred State Ideal Teacher Award by Government of Maharashtra. He has been teaching in St. Francis De Sales College, (RTM Nagpur University) since 1987.

Leela D'Souza, She is Guiding Faculty at the Institute of Indian Culture, Andheri, Mumbai, a Post-graduate Centre for Research in Sociology and Anthropology, recognised by the University of Mumbai.

Manoj Kumar Jha, Associate Professor, Department of Social Work, University of Delhi, Delhi.

Gladson Dungdung, He is a Human Rights Activist and Writer, Ranchi, Jharkhand.

S. Mangi Singh, He is Professor in the Department of Political Science, Manipur University, Manipur, Canchipur, Imphal.

Oinam Jitendra Singh, Faculty, Centre for Human Rights and Duties Education, Manipur University, India.

Mohan Kashikar, Professor, Department of Political Science, RTM Nagpur University, Nagpur.

Ram Puniyani, He is associated with a Communal Harmony group, EKTA, Mumbai, web www.pluralindia.com, ram.puniyani@gmail.com).

Kartik Lokhande, He has been working as Chief Reporter with 'the Hitavada', Nagpur daily for the last 14 years. He has been delivering lecture on Naxalism, Defence Issue and Electoral reforms.

He has travelled extensively in farmers' suicide belt and Naxal-affected areas of Vidharaba region.

Asghar Ali Engineer, He was the director of Centre for Study of Society and Secularism. He was the founder editor of Indian Journal of Secularism.

1

Communal Violence in India: A Crisis of Identity

Leela D'Souza

Introduction

The birth of India as a nation unfortunately coincided with the eruption of communal violence between the Hindu and Muslim communities, which tension had been simmering several years earlier. Today communal violence has taken different expressions, not just between religious communities. It includes ethnic (including tribal), caste, regional and language communities like the demands in Punjab for a separate Khalistan, the struggles in north-east India between tribal communities and non-tribal, the claims of the Shiv Sena and the Maharashtra Navnirman Sena in Maharashtra, which are cases of communal violence.

The increasing incidences of communal violence in recent times can be closely linked to the crisis of identity, that itself is a complex issue. Self-perception is an important factor in creating feelings of fear or threat to self-identity. It can emerge due to one or several factors that operate successively or simultaneously: In times of rapid social change; where economic conflicts and pressures create feelings of insecurity; or where in a democracy the political manipulation of communities add to the perceived threat to self-identity. It can also be linked with perceptions of threat in the context of majority-minority community relations.

The word 'community' arises from the root word, 'commune' means a group of people bound together on some basis (ethnicity, religion and territory). P. Heehs speaks of communalism as a complex phenomenon, whose roots cannot be exposed by tracing its genesis.[1] Communalism is not the same as terrorism, though it is often difficult to sharply distinguish the two, for one often slips into the other and they can overlap. The Naxalite uprising in India may be termed acts of terror, as also the recent attacks by the Sanatan Sanstha in different parts of India. The carnage in Gujarat following the burning of the train at Godhra, could be considered a clash between two religious communities.

Communal Violence in India's Past

In history, communal violence has always existed and clashes between communities/tribes have often resulted in wars. India has been formed as a nation by the bringing together of pre-existing communities of different languages, cultures, historical backgrounds and religions into a common territory. (In post World War I period, in Europe, the unification of territories into nations took place based on language, people and culture, whereas in Asia, including India, the unification of territories into nations took place largely from demands for liberation from colonial rule in a post World War II period. E. Kedourie, H. Kohn, A. Hastings, E. Gellner and others have discussed these processes in detail). The concept of nation is seen by E. Kedourie as imported from Europe and not indigenous to the non-European world. A Smith contrasts between a territorial nationalism as emerged in Europe and an ethnic nationalism which emerged from a need to preserve a cultural identity, as happened in the colonised nations.[2] Huntington sees societies united by ideology or historical circumstance but divided by civilisation either come apart, as did the Soviet Union and Yugoslavia, or subjected to intense strain as in India and Sri Lanka.[3]

It must be remembered that India as a political unit did not exist prior to Independence from the British in 1947. In fact, the British and other colonial powers (Portuguese, Dutch and French) had used the antagonisms and distrust between the different ruling kingdoms and peoples of India to consolidate their control over India. Even later, they played one community against the other in order to maintain their dominance. Political exclusiveness between the Hindus and the Muslims existed even during the freedom struggle, as seen from the fact that no Muslim was on any political organisation or committee. Rather, as soon as the Muslims became politically conscious, they started separate organisations of their own from 1856 onwards.[4] The differences between the two communities were highlighted, when legislation for local self-government was introduced on an elective basis and the Muslims demanded for separate representation as a minority community[5]. The birth of India as a nation in 1947 was marred by such communal distrust, which erupted into violence of unprecedented proportions, the scars of which remain till today.

During the freedom struggle in India, two sharp, divergent views had emerged: One as expressed by the secular, democratic, inclusive forces headed by the Congress under Pandit Jawaharlal Nehru. G.B. Tilak, though ideologically a Hindu nationalist, did not create a Hindu organisation inside or outside the Congress, but instead remained within the Congress Party as an extremist. The other view was expressed by the non-secular, communal, exclusivist camp represented by the Rashtriya Swayamsevak Sangh (RSS) and its ideologues. The formation of the right wing, militant, Hindu political party, the Hindu Mahasabha in 1915, indicated the coming together of politics and religion. They were giving a call for a religious basis for nationalism. The rise of religious nationalism has thus contributed directly to the rise of religious communalism, the idea of Hindu nationalism being constructed between the years 1870-1920.

The fears of being subordinated by the Hindu majority-politically, culturally and economically-led to a crisis of identity by the Muslim minority in India. The demands for a separate political identity in the Muslim majority regions was demanded as early as 1940, as Provincial autonomous regions. The debate over the role of

Muhammad Ali Jinnah during Partition has been recently raised again, in the recent controversy over the statements made by Mr. Jaswant Singh.

Politicisation of religion has continued to erupt in continual, communal violence in India. No doubt the idea of a two-nation theory was encouraged, even supported by the departing British Government, but the fact remains that India has not been able to resolve the hardening differences arising between the Hindu majority community and the Muslim minority community. Communal violence in India continues, which is not only based on religious communalism but also other forms of communal violence based on ethnic, language and regional criteria. Though the immediate reasons may differ in the different cases, one of the major underlying causes is a crisis of identity as perceived by a community.

Communal Violence in Recent Times

Hindu-Muslim Violence

With the assassination of Mahatma Gandhi and the subsequent banning of the communal organisation, the RSS, by Sardar Vallabhai Patel, the first Home Minister of free India, communal violence was held in check. Clarifying the facts, Irfan Habib upheld that while Sardar Patel did not hold the RSS guilty of the assassination of Gandhiji, he held it responsible for creating the communal atmosphere that led to the assassination.[6] The initial, turbulent years of India as a nation saw no major issues of communal violence and Pandit Nehru, with his emphasis on 'unity in diversity', his astute leadership and a strongly emphasised secular, democratic, inclusive basis for India, managed to steer India on the path of economic growth and development through the Five Year Plans, the Green Revolution, Panchayat Rule, Tribal Development Approach and so on. Many of the controversies that emerged at this early period were settled without too much conflict, except perhaps the demands of the south for a separate Dravidistan, on the basis of resentment of imposition of Hindi as the national language. Other dissenting issues like the Privy Purse and the re-organisation of States on basis of ethnic/language/cultural lines were managed effectively and contained any potential communal clashes. This thrust of Pandit Nehru of Unity in Diversity is being seriously challenged today.

The constant appeasement of the minority Muslim community by the Congress as perceived by the RSS, led to a perceived threat by the majority Hindu community. The decades of the 1980s and 1990s saw the emergence of a powerful right wing of Hindu movement in India. In 1980 the Jan Sangh changed its image to the Bharatiya Janata Party and in 1984, the Bajrang Dal, a militant wing of the Vishwa Hindu Parishad was formed. In the 1984 general elections, the BJP won a mere two seats, but five years later it won 86 seats. In 1990, the BJP pursued the old demand, first politically exploited by the Hindu Mahasabha in the 1850s and reactivated in 1949[7] to construct a 'Mandir' at Ayodhya on the site where Babur had constructed a mosque in 1528. It announced the Rath Yatra to be led by Mr. L.K. Advani, from the ancient temple of Somnath in Gujarat to Ayodhya in U.P., the claimed birth place of Ram, and so symbolically liberate India for the Hindus. It was hoped that the Yatra would consolidate the Hindu vote and capture power at the centre. The destruction of the Babri Masjid at Ayodhya on December 6, 1992 on the basis of the Hindutva ideology once again ignited fears in the Muslim minority community and resulted in religious communal violence. India has subsequently suffered several attacks by the Taliban and its allied fundamentalist forces—the attack on Parliament, the bomb blasts in the trains of Mumbai to name just a few–as a continued Muslim response to the fundamentalist, hard-line, Hindutva ideology. The response of the Sanatan Sanstha, a Hindu fundamentalist organisation, to the Muslim fundamentalist forces, is a dangerous political development to peace and harmony in India.

(a) Violence against Christians

The perceived threat by the Hindutva forces to its identity in India has led it to unleash atrocities, often inhuman, against Christians. The brutal burning of Graham Staines and his two young sons in Odisha in January 1999, the recent attacks in December 2007 against the tribals in the Kandhmal district of Odisha, are two prominent cases. But persistent destruction and burning of churches in different parts of India continue. The Catholic

Secular Forum has reported an increase in atrocities against Christians in 2011 that has doubled from 2010 and has covered nearly all States in the country, with Karnataka and Odisha being the States with the largest number of attacks.[8] Today, we are experiencing not just the stranglehold of democracy by mobocracy, but we are also experiencing the usurpation of India's identity by the Hindutva brigade, falsely claiming India to be a Hindu nation. In reality, India is a nation of diverse identities-ethnic, religious, language and regional.[9]

(b) Sikh Identity

The demand for a separate Sikh identity and subsequently for a separate, sovereign Sikh nation, began as early as the 1920s and grew in force after Independence, when the Sikhs began perceiving a threat to their identity as a separate religious group from the majority Punjabi Hindu population, with which they were being closely identified. Tat (true) Khalsa reformers sought to reinforce a Sikh identity, clearly distinct from a Hindu identity. Hindu politicians on the other hand did not see this as a legitimate demand, as they saw Sikhs as Hindus. The active work of the Arya Samaj, founded by Swami Dayanand Saraswati, in Punjab, further increased the perceived threat by the Sikhs to their identity.

In Independent India, Sikhs felt they were of little political consequence, but as a distinct minority group they would get recognition. Separatism from Hindus became a political platform on which to establish a distinct Sikh identity and consciousness. This was the demand of the Akali Dal, the political wing of the Shiromani Gurudwara Prabhandak Committee (SGPC), formed as a result of the Sikh Gurudwara Act, 1925. The demand for Sikh nationalism can be traced back to the latter part of the nineteenth century, when Punjab was annexed by the British in 1849.[10]

During the struggle for Independence, the Akali Dal persistently demanded for separate electoral representation for the Sikhs. After Independence they demanded for the formation of a separate Sikh State, which was granted in 1966 by the State Reorganisation Committee, where Sikh Punjabis were in a majority with about 54 per cent of the population of the State, the Hindu Punjabis forming only 44 per cent of the population.[11] The call for a separate

Sikh nation had been voiced from the 1920s, but by 1981 Harchand Singh Longowal, President of the working committee of the Akali Dal, reiterated the call for the implementation of the Anandpur Sahib resolution of 1973, which called for the formation of a Sikh nation.[12] The continued fears of being absorbed by Brahmanical traditions and the emergence of fundamentalist, extremist forces led by Jarnail Singh Bhindranwale, arose to make forceful demands for a Sikh nation-Sikhistan or Khalistan. By 1983, the extremists began indiscriminate killings of Hindus in the State to create fear among the Hindu population, which would lead to an exodus of Punjabi Hindus from the State.[13] In 1984, Operation Bluestar by the Army at the Golden Temple to flush out Bhindranwale and other extremists holed up in the Akal Takht and other areas of the Golden Temple, was seen as a desecration of the Temple and a deliberate attempt to humiliate the community, rather than as a necessary step to curb violence The retaliatory assassination of Mrs. Indira Gandhi in October 1984 by her own Sikh bodyguards and the brutal anti-Sikh riots that followed, allegedly at the instigation of some Congress leaders, led to a sense of deep alienation of the Sikh community. Today, the extremist elements in the Sikh leadership have been silenced and with both the SGPC and the Akali Dal enjoying electoral control in the State, the Sikhs have begun to recognise themselves as an integral part of India.

(c) Communal Violence in the North East

The national spirit in India was formed as a result of the struggle for Independence against the colonial powers. Diverse communities came together for this single purpose. Once India gained freedom and emerged as a nation, the 'fault-lines' on which the nation was formed began manifesting themselves. (The term 'fault-lines' was first used by Samuel Huntington, (1997: 207-208). These new tensions in India need to be seen in the context of the political maturity of India as a democracy. The proposals of the Mandal Commission that was constituted in 1978, but implemented only in 1990 by the Government led by Mr. V. P. Singh, gave power to the OBCs and middle level castes. The Congress had managed to retain power based on an upper caste/untouchable/minority vote (Brahmin/Dalit/Muslim). 'Mandalisation' encouraged the OBCs to fight for a separate identity and a share in governance. This has resulted in the creation of new ethnic and caste groups forming political parties to contest elections in States, as happened in U.P., Bihar, Odisha, Tamil Nadu and other States. New majority-minority conflicts have arisen with the tendency of the newly formed political parties to politicise issues on the basis of religion, ethnicity, caste and language, causing new bases of communal violence in India. In the north-east also, local/regional parties have emerged with the tendency to politicise identities on a single ethnic basis.

At Independence, the political boundaries of the north east were arbitrarily constructed, leaving uncertain grey zones, disputed territories and discontented peoples, demanding various degrees of autonomy or independence. In 1946, the Governor of Assam, Sir Akbar Hydari, entered into an accord with the Naga National Council, giving them the right to 'to develop themselves according to their freely expressed wishes' in all judicial, fiscal and cultural matters, adding that after ten years, the Naga National Council would be given the option to extend the accord if they so wished or re-negotiate it. Not unexpectedly, the Government of Independent India did not take any notice of this agreement. Insurgency and counter-insurgency operations have followed in the succeeding years.[14] Majumdar mentions that after the Anglo-Burmese war in 1826, Burma was forced to remove its supremacy over all the north-eastern States, after which the British took over the administration of these territories.[15]

A similar view is expressed M. S. Prabhakara who states that in the north east even in the post 1947 period, the expression of 'Assamese Nation' was maintained alongside the idea of 'Indian Nation'. One response to the popular resistance in these regions was the re-organisation of the north-east on a linguistic basis,[16] which occurred after the war with China in 1962. In response to the Naga insurgency and the demands for Naga self-rule, the Government in 1963 established the State of Nagaland. In 1966, the Mizos of the Mizo Hills district of Assam rebelled, in response to which the district was converted into a Union Territory in 1972 and subsequently into a full-fledged state. The Northeast Frontier agency, created in 1954 out of the North East Frontier Tracts (one of the 'excluded areas' of colonial Assam), was given its own legislature in

1969, made a Union Territory in 1972 and subsequently established as a separate State of Arunachal Pradesh in 1987. Today there are seven separate states in the north-east-Assam, Arunachal Pradesh, Mizoram, Manipur, Nagaland, Tripura and Meghalaya.[17] Bodos are now still demanding for a separate Bodoland. The Gorkha National Liberation Front (in Darjeeling) is a form of ethnic assertion based on a Nepalese-Indian Identity.[18] These steps, instead of containing the separatist demands in these regions, has instead led to regionalism taking on more complicated forms, where the earlier call for Indian nationalism has now transferred itself to ethno-nationalism.[19] For example, in Mizoram, after the 1996 polls, differences between the tribal components of Mizoram started gaining greater expression. Today, the Chakma issue simmers and the demand of the Hmars are gaining momentum.[20]

The reasons for such separatist demands are fuelled more out of a crisis of identity-the fear and hatred of 'the other'. Today, these tribal communities still feel alienated from India due to several reasons, the main ones being racial differences from the dominant communities of India and distance in physical communication. Further, economic inputs have led to growth of cities and economic opportunities have led to migration to these cities from neighbouring areas, especially from West Bengal, Bihar and even Bangladesh. Tribals see this numerical input into 'their State' as a threat to their territorial and political space and they also feel economically and socially threatened. This has led to increasing communal violence against whom they perceive as 'outsiders'. The ULFA, (United Liberation Front of Asom) has emerged as the political voice of these demands of the ethnic communities of Assam. Today, these demands are being politicised by local leaders, who are inciting fear and hatred of 'the other' and also emphasising a single basis for identity-ethnicity.

(d) Maharashtra

Movements of 'ethnic cleansing' can also be seen in Maharashtra today, as expressed by the Shiv Sena and its offshoot, the Maharashtra Navnirman Sena (MNS), who are demanding for greater economic opportunities to the 'sons of the soil'. After the debacle of Uddhav Thackeray at 2009 Assembly elections, he has promised that the Shiv Sena will not be found lacking in forcefully expressing the demands/protecting the interests of Maharashtrians.

The Shivaji festival which was started by B. G. Tilak in 1895, sought to portray Shivaji as a liberator of Maharashtra and a protector of Hinduism.[21] This move by Tilak did not meet with much success during his lifetime, but in recent years it was appropriated by late Shree Bal Thackery, founder of the Shiv Sena in 1966. In the initial years, much hatred was directed to the South Indians in Mumbai, who Late Shree Bal Thackeray claimed were taking away jobs from the 'natives'. According to Anupama Katakam, the Shiv Sena never had any lofty ideology and was made up mostly of lumpen elements. It went from strength to strength by propagating communal hate. Now the MNS has stolen its 'ideology' and operates in much the same manner.[22]

Search for Identity

These and other expressions of communal violence like the struggle between the Mina and Gujjar communities in Rajasthan, seem to be an expression of a crisis of identity in a period we can call 'beyond modernisation', which period overlaps with the period of globalisation. As the old bases of community in traditional India-joint family, caste, village Panchayat-are being replaced by new bases of identity in an industrialised, urbanised context, the previous homogenous, stable identities of a traditional society are being replaced by pluralistic, flexible, even conflicting identities in the modern context.

The search for identity is a natural phenomenon for any individual, community and nation. It is the basis of self-understanding based on distinct characteristics that separate one from the other. Identity is the basis of existence, of bonding together in a feeling of belongingness, of sense of community, which is essential for the building up of self, community and nation. The symbols of the national flag, the national anthem, the Constitution, are all symbols of identity building as a nation. Each cultural group has a distinct identity and each group interacts with others at certain intersecting points or meeting points. Yet each maintains distinct identities. Today unfortunately there is a tendency to establish closed and rigid identities, where meeting points are points of disagreement or clash with the other.

The building of self-identity implies distinctiveness from other. This is the in-built dichotomy for the existence of identity-I-You; we-them; in group-out group. Difference from 'other' is the basis of identity. Thus while on the one hand identity formation has a positive role to play in building up self/community/nation, on the negative side, stress on identity could lead to distancing oneself from the 'other'. In India, the basis of such differences are immense-religion, region, language, caste and ethnicity. To overcome such tendencies, stress can be laid on the shared or common points of identities of different communities. In the context of a modernised, pluralistic society, construction of identity is in the context of multiple others, where boundaries often overlap over several criteria. Multi-culturalism or pluralism is nothing new to India. It has existed from India's ancient period.

In sociological terms, identity is something constructed, fluid, multiple and changing. In traditional, homogenous societies, identity was static, integral, unified and even given. In modern societies identities need to get constructed and re-constructed on an on-going basis. Threat to or loss of a traditional identity often results in a cultural vacuum, leading to a reassertion of origins or traditional identity.[23] In this context, the demand for identity often takes on a political hue, where only one aspect of a pluralistic identity is emphasised and becomes the rallying basis for members, to the denial/subordination of the other parts of multiple identities. Thus Muslims, Hindus, Gujjars, Assamese, Sikhs, Maharashtrian become the sole identity-rallying points. Such a singular emphasis in a pluralistic identity may not involve the entire community, but often a vociferous minority becomes more expressive and active, who seek to assert their right to the identity of the entire community. The community may quietly support them, because of the alleged benefits that will accrue to the entire community. Persons respond to such an emphasis because of a perceived threat/feeling of economic insecurity/social insecurity of a minority community or other felt need.

This pattern of creating hatred towards the other and an emphasis on only one aspect of a multiple identity, which is more often done for political gain, can be overcome by providing economic benefits, so that economic insecurity does not facilitate the communal forces. As Imtiaz Ahmad, a great Political, sociologist from JNU, has pointed out, the focus needs to be on sharing of overlapping identities to maintain communal harmony. Mobility of identity must be recognised and that existing configurations can be re-drawn.[24] We need to remind ourselves that we have several identities and not allow ourselves to be boxed into a single identity.

Identity is formed not in isolation but in the context of a culture, of shared memories, a shared history. The cultural background into which one is born is internalised and forms both the basic collective identity of a people and the basic individual identity of a person. Today, this can and does change progressively as external circumstances change. What is relevant today in the context of multi-cultural societies, is not the creation of an identity but the recycling of an identity in order to accommodate 'the other'.

In the Indian context, while 'differences' need to be allowed, even encouraged, since this is the basic reality of India, the 'other' needs to be consciously included into the 'self image' and a new inclusive self image created that tolerates the other.[25] As Richardson has commented, globalisation need not result in a 'sameness', but in a willingness to accept the 'differences' of the other. Progressive identity can only be achieved through cultural receptiveness and reciprocity by both the 'us' and the 'they' components. The 'other' must also seek to be accepted, so that sharp differences can be tapered off. Ways and means need to be found to express one's own identity without in any way impinging on or diminishing that of the 'other'.

Why Violence?

Violence seems to be the increasing norm adopted by communities, who feel their demands are not being met. When there is a perception of threat to the identity of a community and the community gets organised to protect its rights/interests, once organised, it may turn to violence as a means to meet its demands. But why violent take place? What are the reasons these cultural differences form to a point of extreme intolerance of the 'other', leading even to violence? Political manipulation of a single identity for the sake of garnering votes is a prime cause of communal violence. Recent example can be seen Muzaffarnagar communal violence committed by local parties. Politics today is manipulating these multiple communities along the 'fault lines' of the Indian nation, emphasising a singular basis of identity, allowing other common bases of identity to be subordinated. This is an unreal situation, since individuals belong to multiple identities. Huntington had observed that identities tend to become hardened along communal lines. Political leaders expand and deepen their appeals to specific loyalties, either ethnic or religious. A 'hate' dynamic emerges where mutual fears, distrust and hatred feed on each other. Moderates, with more limited goals do not achieve their ends through negotiation and so radicals take over and seek to achieve more extreme goals through violence.[26]

Today the norm seems to be emerging that a minority group that has less bargaining power across the table, can express its demands more forcefully through violence. Concern is not given that these means are against the democratic, secular principles of the nation or that they are demands for exclusive status for a region, which are contrary to constitutional provisions. In these days of global interaction, such demands may be counter-productive both to the community demanding it and to India as a nation.

This is a revised version her article published in Social Action Vol. 60, Jan-March 2010.

References

1. Heehs, P. (2006). Nationalism, Terrorism, Communalism. Delhi. Oxford University Press, p. 9.
2. D'Souza, Leela. 2002 'Ethnic Nationalism in India: An Appraisal' *Vidyajyoti*, Vol. 66, No. 1, pp. 36-38.
3. Huntington, S.P., (1997) *The Clash of Civilisations and the Remarking of world Order*. New Delhi. Penguin Books India (P) Ltd., p. 28.
4. Majumdar, R.C., (1965) 'Muslim Community', in R.C. Majumdar (ed.) *British Paramountcy and Indian Renaissance II*. Vol. X. Bombay, Bharatiya Vidya Bhavan, p. 297.
5. *Ibid.*, p. 302.
6. Neena Vyas, (2009) 'Sardar Patel banned RSS under pressure from Nehru: Advani, *the Hindu* August; 22, p. 14.
7. Jaffrelot, C., (1996) *The Hindu Nationalist Movement and Indian Politics. 1925-1990s*. New Delhi. Viking, pp. 91-92.

8. Times News Network, 'Maharashtra among 10 states where Christians attacked' in *Times of India*, January 12, 2012, p. 10.
9. D'Souza, Leela, 2007. *Cultural History of Ancient India. Diversity, Syncretism, Synthesis*. Jaipur, Rawat Publications, pp. 8-16.
10. Kapur, R.A., 1986. Sikh Separatism. *The Politics of Faith*. London. Allen & Unwin Publishers Ltd. xii-xv; Majumdar, R.C. (1963). 'Rise and Fall of Sikh Kingdom' in R.C. Majumdar (ed.) *British Paramountcy and Indian Renaissance I*. Vol. IX. Bombay. Bharatiya Vidya Bhavan, p. 235.
11. Kapur, R.A., 1986. *Sikh Separatism. The Politics of Faith*. London. Allen & Unwin Publishers Ltd., p. 216.
12. *Ibid.*, pp. 219-220.
13. *Ibid.*, pp. 226-227.
14. Pandey, G. and Yunus Samad, 2007. *Fault-lines of Nationhood*. Delhi. Lotus Collection. Roli Books, p. 56.
15. Majumdar, R.C., 1965. '*Muslim Community*' in R. C. Majumdar (ed.) *British Paramountcy and Indian Renaissance II*. Vol. X. Bombay. Bharatiya Vidya Bhavan. pp, 129-335.
16. Prabhakara, M.S. 2009. '*Ethno-nationalism: theory and practice*' The Hindu, October 28, p. 8.
17. Pandey, G. and Yunus Samad, 2007. *Fault-lines of Nationhood*. Delhi. Lotus Collection. Roli Books, p. 57.
18. Verghese, B.G., 1997, *India's North-east Resurgent. Ethnicity, Insrgency, Governance, Development*. New Delhi, Konark Publishers Pvt. Ltd., p. 292.
19. Prabhakara, M.S., 2009. '*Ethno-nationalism: theory and practice*' The Hindu, October 28, p. 8.
20. Verghese, 1997 op. cit., p. 409.
21. Majumdar, R.C., 1965. '*Muslim Community*' in R. C. Majumdar (ed.) *British Paramountcy and Indian Renaissance II*. Vol. X. Bombay. Bharatiya Vidya Bhavan, pp. 295-579.
22. Katakam, A. 2009. '*Wounded Tiger*' in Frontline, Vol. 26, No. 23, November 20, p. 16.
23. Ahmad, Imtiaz. 2003. '*Identity and Nationalism: Historical Roots and Contemporary Manifestations*'. Social Action. Vol. 53, No. 4, p. 429. Also see, D'Souza, Leela. 2003. '*Identity Formation and Pluralism: The Need to Reconstruct Identities*'

Social Action, Vol. 53, No. 4, pp. 422-428.

24. Ahmad, Imtiaz, op. cit.
25. Richardson, M. 2001. *The Experience of Culture*. New Delhi. Sage Publications, p. 172.
26. Huntington, S.P., 1997. *The Clash of Civilisations and the Remaking of Word Order*. New Delhi. Penguin Books India (P) Ltd., p. 266.

2

Living Together Separately: Ritualised Riots and the Disparaged Others

Manoj Kumar Jha

I am conscious of the fact that the following lines shall be read and scrutinised in the wake of a decade of Gujarat riots 2002; a decade which has seen continued mourning not only by victims and survivours but by a large section of civil society. More than ten years since then have also resulted in more of despair and hopelessness for the victims, survivours as well as for all those who are concerned about the shrinking width of secular democratic space. The progression of gloominess also has its roots in largely unattended and unhealed wounds compounded by the ever increasing distance between the victims and their hopes for justice. Before we choose to proceed further, it is pertinent to ask-can India survive amongst the civilised nations of the world live with this kind of stigmatisation of a particular section of her populace? Can India translate its lofty constitutional ideals of secular living into reality? The tenor of the exhortation coming out from certain political parties and a vocal section of the media does not allow us to have much faith in defending diversity in our context. Besides if such hate rhetoric goes unopposed it might see further rise of authoritarian and blatant misuse of political power at the one end and the rise of exclusivist philosophy on the other. So far episodes of violence between religious communities have generally been explained as symptomatic of a society which has 'forgotten' the skills of plural living and togetherness. The overwhelming presence, persona and stature of contemporary narratives of violence seem to corroborate this view even though violent outbursts are not new to the Indian landscape. Herein, attempt shall be made to place the riots in the larger context of rapidly changing nature of the spaces in which human beings chose to interact or remain oblivious of each other. It also aims at placing the larger frames of violence and the violent structures besides the smaller frame of gradual but systematic reduction in the size of the moral community. An endeavour shall also be made to problematise the simplistic interpretation of any act of violence as occurring between persons identified as belonging to different religious groups. While that may remain the context (that of two competing and antagonistic religious communities in situations of violence) there are agencies like — the media, states' machinery and other (ethnic/social) neutral categories; whose testimony and account of the violence has far wider implications at times, than the victims or the participants. Redrawing of the contours of inter-community relations in a way began in the late 1980s through Khurja, Bijnor, Bhagalpur and Mumbai. The modernisation of the instruments and agencies of violence in Gujarat 2002 indicated complicity of ever larger constituencies drawn from diverse contexts and situations. One of the central hallmarks of the violence in last two decades can be seen as to how the participants in the organised killings were accorded high ritual status and how conveniently they could get away with the crime committed against humanity. The Action Take Report including the intent of the ruling regime explicitly shows the dissolution of the distinction between civility and barbarity. It also goes as natural adjunct to a situation crafted by the Sangh Parivar, wherein political, social and religious groups employ the instrument of violence against an almost defenceless victim without being apologetic about it in anyway.

The submission of the voluminous report of the Liberhan[1] Commission and the consequent noise and contentious positions impels us to look at the fragmentation of the communities and societies in recent times. It also wants us to look at the divergent frames of the private and the public memory before and after the demolition of the Babri Masjid seventeen years back. The available social data undoubtedly underlines that greatest of the violent episodes in recent times have occurred when the criminal aggression got 'ritualised'; meaning thereby that the perpetrators had nothing to fear and nothing to feel bad, for it was all intrinsically devised as set of rituals and supposedly with the consensus of a majority. The vanishing lines between ritualised violence and brutal criminal violence indicate a major shift in the socio-cultural framework governing distnatiation and consequently, the formation of the disparaged or dehumnaised others. In fact, the agitation which was led from the front by the VHP/BJP and RSS leaders witnessed substantial ruptures in inter-community relations in almost every part of India. Expression of violence; brute physical and the psychological ones were just the natural corollary of a politics which frequently changed the garbs of religion, culture, politics and social reconstruction.

Such crimes and acts of barbarity were committed *en masse* not only in regard to the number of victims, but also in regard to the numbers of those who perpetuated the crime, and the extent to which anyone of the many criminals was close to or remote from the actual killer of the victims means nothing, as far as the measure of his responsibility is concerned. On the contrary, in general the degree of responsibility, it increases as we draw further away from the man who uses the fatal instrument with his own hands. This is one of the main points that Hannah Arendt[2] emphasises throughout her report. She did not think that prosecution had proved "beyond a reasonable doubt" that Eichmann had committed an overt act of murder "with his own hands." She strongly objected to what she took to be the prosecutor's melodramatic attempt to demonise Eichmann to portray him as a "sadistic monster" who was possessed by an "insane hatred of the Jews". By relying on such conventional categories, the prosecutor obscured the character of this "desk criminal" and his crimes. She highlights that Eichmann was neither "perverted nor sadistic". He was "terrifyingly normal." And the perpetration of most barbaric and brutal violence since the mid 1980s in India was built around the vortex of terrifyingly normal persons. The victims appeared defenceless and numb on account of the fact that actual physical violence followed the subterranean ideological work by the Sangh parivar which meticulously aimed at othering of certain communities from the private as well as the public realm in localities. Ironically, studies on the mass and organised killings have been marred by a poor understanding and an under-theorising of *othering and distantiation*. Othering is a broad, typically imprecisely used term, encompassing a wide variety of processes and the phenomena. This naturally poses enormous obstacles for explaining the perpetration of the mass killing because a central task of any such attempt is to evaluate whether and how the ideology of othering and distantiation produced and influenced its many aspects, the way it did.

Most of the explanations coming in the wake of progression of violent episodes in reality caricature the perpetrators, i.e., those who chose to participate in the mayhem since the opening of the lock at the disputed structure. The accounts treat them as if they had been people lacking the ability to decide a moral sense, lacking the ability to make decisions and take stances. They do not conceive of the actors as human agents, as people with wills, but as being moved solely by external forces or by transhistorical and invariant psychological propensities such as the slavish following of narrow self interest.

The conventional explanations available for the progression of the violent episodes in the decades following the opening of the lock at the disputed structure at Faizabad also suffer from further conceptual obscurity. Even before the submission of the Liberhan Commission reports, there was no dearth of detailed narratives of the accounts of the death and destruction drawn on diverse episodes of violence from all over India, they in fact fall much short of underlining the extraordinary nature of the act, i.e., the distantiation followed by mass killing and destruction of the *disparaged others*.

Drawing from the writings of Staub (2007), Waller (2007) and Goldhagen (1997) in the context of Nazi Germany, we have reasons including the substantial empirical evidence which suggests that we should not undermine the actors' nee perpetrators' capacity to understand, apprise and judge and it should also take into account their own personal negotiations with morality and moral framework of connectedness. It needs to be recognised that we were a normal society or even there were certain abnormal tendencies they had been available more or less in the same quantity. Hence what made people agree and willing to distantiate (at cognitive as well as spatial level) the *disparaged others* requires a different structure and frame of understanding.

While talking of the nature of evil, Waller[3] says, 'In general conversation, we easily substitute "moral wrongness" or "bad" for the term "evil" without any loss of meaning. Some see "evil" as grandiose, and others find it esoteric, mystical or supernatural. For most of us, the "evil" is an antiquated concept. It is a relic heavy with archaic baggage (for example, the notion of sin). In short, though we know it from fairy tales, children's books, comic books, horror films, "evil" is a word modern folk do not often hear or use.

Even those authors and scholars, who derive and make their arguments on the basis of religion and philosophy, do not actually define "evil". What Waller highlights that, 'to specifically define the "judgmental" and "moralistic" concept of evil seems to threaten the academic ideal of ethical and value neutrality. To be sure, any definition includes, in part, a value statement reflecting one's own perspective. Following in the arguments of James Waller, we can have a working/operational definition of human evil as the deliberate harming of human by other humans. As this is a behavioural definition, that focuses on how people act toward one another. This definition of human evil includes the creation of conditions that materially or psychologically destroy or diminish people's quality of life-their dignity, happiness and capacity to fulfil basic material needs. Such conditions aim to threaten or impact socio-cultural as well as economic and political realms of the *disparaged others*. It belittles their persona, pushes them further on the margins and shuts them out of the corridor without allowing them any space for speaking out whatever anguish they have.

The Psychology of Perpetrators: Individuals and the Cultural System

To understand the psychology of perpetrators, we must consider their persona, the forces acting on them, and the system they are part of. The cultural system makes one of the most pervasive impact on the persona of all known by the differential categories such as perpetrators, onlookers, bystanders and the witnesses through selective overemphasis on specific items in the worldview. A worldview, according to Waller[4] includes the presuppositions, intentions, meanings, rules, norms, values, principles, practices, and activities through which people live their lives. It is a fundamental orientation that includes the core cultural ideals of what is good and what is moral. Implied in this *distantiating* worldview is the obliteration of a common ground between perpetrators and victims and between the wounded and the witnesses as well as the bystanders. Meticulously built aggression towards the *others* consequently transcends the boundaries of the moral framework governing inter-personal and *inter-community* relations. The innermost aspects of *distantiation* can be seen in the manner in which we come across newer spaces increasingly appearing witness to minor altercation being transmogrified into between the criminal elements of both the communities and at times amongst the rival factions within the same community. In the recent past preceding the Ramshila Pujan, violence had entered from the larger frame to the everyday behaviour of the communities and consequently there were increased physical expressions to the animosities and differences. The Mukhiya of the village was notorious for his criminal proclivities and the dislike for his activities notwithstanding, he enjoyed substantial muscle power and that found a willing VHP for courtship. The villagers also informed that the Mukhiya ran extortion and kidnapping gang and had affiliations within and beyond the district. In the years preceding the riot of 1989, there were stray cases of feud involving the goons of the Mukhiya and a few members of the Muslim community; which the Mukhiya unsuccessfully tried to represent as on account of divergent religious identity. Later on, conflicting interest over the adjacent plots of land brought another brawl into open. But in this case too, Mukhiya's endeavour could never get on to become a frame of communal violence in Bhattoria. However, the Mukhiya kept on nurturing and cementing his political ambitions while deliberately creating wedges between the communities in the village. At this stage VHP entered the village with its flagship Shilapujan programme and the criminal Mukhiya soon had the makeover and appeared as one of the important members of the VHP in his locality committed to the construction of a magnificent Ram temple at Ayodhya. Politicised religion and its rituals perform diverse set of functions and one of them is no matter how much of sin the recruited ones have committed in the past, they are not to be pushed away from God, at least in the collective memory of people around. Participation with vigour and dedication in the public theatre of politicised religion in effect allows them to have recompense come quickly and readily for them. And consequently Bhattoria too changed and transformed, it was no more the Bhattoria people knew for so long. It had differences and altercations always between individuals and communities but they were never approached with the lens of the political-religious identity of the communities involved. However, this new Bhattoria in a short span of time had developed tremendous capacity in signifying an existing irritant between two individuals (belonging to two different communities) as ready case in point of *intrinsic incompatibilities* of the two religions. There were several villagers informing us that with the ostentatious celebrations of the Ramshila Pujan in the village any possibility of rapprochement between the communities was lost forever. The preparations for the celebration itself caused pain and suffering to the Muslim members of the village in many ways, for in all the preparatory meetings before the celebration, local issues and irritants were presented, discussed and analysed through the communal lenses. These issues were conveyed as the replica of an all-India context, where Muslims were the greatest internal and external threat for India and Indians. With continuous dress rehearsals, Bhattoria was an ideal-typical village with adequate number of willing ears and disposed minds to carry out the task expected of them. Volkan's (1997) *Chosen trauma* and *Chosen glory* had become integral ingredient of the borders and boundaries between the communities. And hence during the same period, when some Muslim criminals were killed by the police in a nearby locality, it is alleged that some of the Muslim families mourned. The Muslims of the Badki Bhattoria as well as English Bhattoria therefore apprehended danger as soon as the news of the rioting reached on 24th October, 1989. In desperation, several families had shifted from English Bhattoria to Badki Bhattoria or to the nearby villages with greater number of Muslims therein. Still there was a large chunk of populace which either could not or did not move out. Many of them did not move out, for they had a very strong conviction that their neighbours shall remain their greatest guards and shields in case of any attack from any quarter.

On the 25th October, English Bhattoria was attacked from by the rampaging mobs led by the same Mukhiya whose claim to fame was briefly discussed above. In the ferocious attack which went on for hours almost as a sport, wherein with every moment the reluctant ones as well as the onlookers were joining the killing spree. They did not take much time in establishing an instant chord with the crowd which had a maypole (Volkan: 1997) in the Mukhiya. More than thirty five people were killed in the attack and the majority of the victims happened to be old men, women and children.

However, the ones who had left for Badki Bhattoria with the hope that being part of the larger Muslim locality, they shall escape the wrath of the co-villagers had greater disappointment in store for them. The crowd with insatiable desire for more blood turned towards Badki Bhattoria in the night of 24th October itself. In view of the size of the tola, the preparation from the killing crowd was equally big and meticulous and in a span of over four hours there were not less than six attacks resulting in injuries and burns and damage to property. Thoroughly dissatisfied with this, there were hectic parleys and the crowd was given the much needed self assurance that a bigger attack shall be undertaken later.

It was part of the folk information that some of the saner elements in the district administration had sense the precarious inter-community situation and had sent a magistrate and an Assistant Sub-Inspector on 25th 1989 October itself from Nathnagar PS. However, the police convoy which started from Nathnagar PS on 25th was meant to reach the site within half an hour at the most could manage to arrive on 26th evening. It shall not be futile to indicate that Bhattoria is located at a distance of two kilometres from Nathnagar.

On the morning of 27th October, the then DIG came over to appraise himself of the situation and did not take time in sensing the brewing tensions between the communities and consequently alerted the policemen and the magistrate on duty there. Barely could he have reached Nathnagar, when Badki Bhattoria was attacked by a three thousand strong mob again under the leadership of the

Mukhiya. The mob had drawn people from Bhattoria as well as from the nearby villages; the police initially tried halting the mob but they quickly left the site and allowed the rioting mob to go ahead in their task of death and destruction for the Muslims in Badki Bhattoria. The annihilation drive against the Muslim residents of the village continued for the whole day and the police men watched the scene gleefully from a nearby village- Zamin-Daryapur where they had conveniently located themselves.

The DIG arrived in the evening the same day to take stock of the situation and to his utter dismay he found the entire tola was razed, causing the death of twenty five persons in all. Three members of a family were roasted alive and an old man was set on fire while he was sleeping. Gujarat 2002 was yet to come but the new India was writing the prologue for more of the genocidal violence which was likely to surface in the coming years. The dead have long gone so have the diminutive protests which were raised against such total violence but a bigger question remains in the psyche of the children (who could manage to survive) are adults now. And the question lurks-what has been done to retrieve the Bhattoria which was lost in 1989? How many Bhattorias have been lost forever since then?

Like the Germans during the Nazi regime, people here also shared the life problems and culture that gave them a common inclination, a societal tilt, to experience certain ways of fulfilling them. The earliest Nazis probably had characteristics that intensified these needs and desires-a wish to relinquish a burdensome identity, authority orientation, anti-Semitism-and that made the means of their satisfaction offered by Hilter especially congenial Doctors in particular may have been attracted to the "biological" aspect of Nazi ideology and its scientific racism.

Demonisation

Before the desire of the dehumanisation/demonisation gets a favourable climate, the tendency to dichotomise the world into us and them is underway. As Staub (1959) says, 'the ties that bind people to significant ingroups are much stronger than this: Deep affective associations, shared understandings, common goals and the perception of a shared fate.' Consequently enemy groups i.e. those outside of our in-groups are created and categorised by an emerging ideology, usually on the basis of cultural devaluation. Consequently, dehumanisation appears as a psychological process whereby the in-group views the other as less than human and thus not deserving of moral consideration. The accounts of the perpetrators and the bystanders of the riots during the span of the Ramjanm Bhoomi agitation bear testimony of the completed cycle of demonisation and that is one important reason that it never appeared as morally outrageous to any significant populace. Protracted conflict not only strains relationships beyond repair, such conditions often lead to feelings of intense hatred and alienation among the groups. Once moral exclusion of the other is complete, the killing or the destruction has to negotiate only with the statutory and legal framework, which of course shall operate within the altered moral framework of the society. Robert Sternberg moves further and underlines underneath the demonisation of others as prerequisite to their decimation, lies the subterranean ideology of hate which is carefully nurtured and shaped in order to accomplish ends that are mindfully, planfully and systematically conceived. In his conceptual model, Sternberg suggests three components of hate. The first, negation of intimacy, involves the seeking of distance from a target group. This component of hate is affective; it is experienced as a negative emotion. The second component, passion, expresses itself motivationally as intense anger or fear in response to a threat. The final component, decision/commitment, is characterised by cognitions of devaluation and diminution toward the target group. This is the cognitive component that is often nurtured by institutions. Dehumanisation starts at the point when, thanks to the distantiation, the objects at which the bureaucratic operation is aimed can and are, reduced to a set of quantitative measures. Dehumanised objects cannot possibly possess a "cause", much less a "just" one; they have no "interests" to be considered, indeed no claim to subjectivity. A strong identification with the same leads to social death i.e. the natural death which follows subsequently is merely a corollary-anticipated and desired one!

Ritualised Riots

The expressions of violence which concerned people at large in the wake of the Ramjanm bhoomi agitation was crafted around the perceptions of each others' identity between the two communities. It believed that conflict can be caused by accentuating the feelings of threat for the majority community and by further highlighting the Muslims as disparaged others. Such threat perceptions were drawn from the mythical version of a tense past, an unresolved or knotty loss in the public memory. Rituals are associated with and are performed according to given set of rites and happen to be a detailed method laying down procedures for following up. Rituals also channelise the aspirations into expressions of collectivity through a progression of performative acts. Rituals have much more agency and dynamism than what constitutes routine. When rituals are invented and propagated they are likely to generate ritualised minds in ritualised spaces. Participative minds in such altered and designated spaces find arenas where important and critical reality is perched.

How and on what occasions do groups use different types of rituals to create and present a collective identity?

1. On occasions, activities resemble customary practices, albeit conducted with more dramatic flair. Groups affirm their identities through practices that ritualise the routine of everyday life.

Killing, annihilations were always the ideal-typical examples of the violent episodes and there no dearth of them in the episodes of violence we witnessed since the unlocking of the gate at Faizabad. However, there are other facets of violence which have not received attention to the same degree i.e. executing deprivation for disparaged others, prohibiting purchase from their shops, refusing to supply them basic necessities such as milk etc. Besides mental processes: Feelings, attitudes and values that individuals and communities were made to hold, prepared a grounds for eruption, legitimisation and subsequent glorification of violence. Hate, fear and mistrust as driving feelings were deliberately pushed in the cognitive structures by the diverse agencies and instruments of Sangh parivar, which allowed people to classify Muslims as barbaric, uncivilised and disparaged others. If an entire community lacked human values as we have within us, killing and annihilation of disparaged others does not prick community conscience at any significant level. In intense conflict situation communities' sense of "who they are" mixes up with "why they are so" and the plight, the vulnerability, the miseries seen around us are attributed to the disparaged others, making the cycle of dehumanisation complete in all aspects.

We can also look at the way, the leaders of the Hindutava movement tried developing their social, cultural and political aims into a whole. An important contribution comes from Frame theory as used by the analysts of the social movement. Frames, according to Benford and Snow (2006) are "slices of observed, experienced, and/ or recorded 'reality' are assembled, collated and packaged . . . such that a new angle of vision, vantage point, and/or interpretation is provided."

By carefully altering the way the Hindutava movement construed and presented itself, it changed probably forever the discourse between us and them i.e. the other. In the carefully designed frame where the locus of the problem was pre-diagnosed by the organisations through all possible manipulation, attribution (of the blame) came quite naturally to the confirm converts as also to the potential ones. Frame resonance can be defined as the degree to which individuals can identify with the stated positions of a frame; and the extent to which a movement achieves resonance with a wide, diverse audience can largely determine its ultimate success or failure (Babb, 1966). Resonance is a manifestation of what is known as consensus mobilisation, whereby movements "activate individuals who already agree with their views and aims" (Snow and Benford 1988).

Memory Alteration and Imagination Inflation

While mapping the contours of the community it is imperative to locate and delve into the issues of memory and history besides identity at the local level. It is generally understood that for any discernible and disturbing rupture in community relations, the adversaries must have a sense of collective identity about themselves and about others against whom they are supposedly juxtaposed. And in the process of conflict each side believes that the fight is between us and them. Developing a sense of self is an essential part of every individual's evolutionary pattern within the larger community identity. Each person's self-conception is a distinctive combination of several identifications—identifications based on gender, class, sect or religion etc. Although identity of the self may apparently coincide with a particular human being, identities per se are actually much wider than that. In their best perceived sense, identities are collective and they stretch beyond borders created by the states and the governments.

Locating Identity in our times Bauman[5] writes: "In our world of rampant 'individualisation', identities are mixed blessings. They vacillate between a dream and a nightmare, and there is no telling when one will turn into the other. At most times the two liquid modern modalities of identity cohabit, even when located at different levels of consciousness. In a liquid modern setting of life, identities are perhaps the most common, most acute, most deeply felt and troublesome incarnations of *ambivalence*.

Moving little further we also realise that hegemonic superimpositions too create and construct identities for the individuals and the groups. And on account of the pervasive impact of these constructed identities people feel (or are made to feel) injured when other persons sharing their identity are injured or killed. It should be stressed that huge physical distance is no check that the images seen and perceived shall not cross administrative borders and boundaries. Identities are constructed on the basis of various traits and experiences and there are large numbers of players as well engaged in the vocation of identity construction. Several of those characteristics, which are presented as sets of identity markers are in reality open to different reading, interpretation and explanation. Race and skin colour have significantly lost favour as identity markers in our own times.

In the same way, some analysts speak of host of primordial identities as ancient and rigid. This however can be contested taking the evolutionary paradigm of any community. In fact there is no dearth of literature to stress that identity is a social construct with people cajoled to choose a history, common ancestry and shared memory for coming out with a range of differences from others.

Identities are portrayal of the self as also attributes projected on to others. They also indicate not only *who we are* but *what others think of* who we are. Bauman[6] depicts the distinction between choices and free will of some on the one hand and incapacitated others as far as identities are concerned. "Let me note that identification is also a powerful factor in stratification; one of its most divisive and sharply differentiating dimensions. At one pole of the emergent global hierarchy are those who can compose and decompose their identities more or less at will, drawing from the uncommonly large, planet-wide pool of offers. At the other pole are crowded those whose access to identity choice has been barred, people who are given no say in deciding their preferences and who in the end are burdened with identities enforced and imposed by others; identities which they themselves resent but are not allowed to shed and cannot manage to get rid of. Stereotyping, humiliating, dehumanising, stigmatising identities. . . ." Such constructed identities if remain uncontested, can persist for generations creating borders and boundaries between us and them.

We do need to admit that arriving at the foundation of the inter-community relations is a worthwhile aim to pursue irrespective of the hazards and risks it entails and if the process of seeking information touches the core of the people's heart, many corridors of the past as they see are open to us. On the other hand, memory is an interdependent process of remembering and forgetting. Memory is also a label for a diverse set of cognitive capacities by which humans retain information and reconstruct past experiences, usually for present purposes. Memory seems to be a source of knowledge, or perhaps is just retained knowledge. However, when the external stake holders are at work in helping people remember (read manufacturing), remembering is often immersed with emotion-a heightened passion; an irrational one as we have seen in our times. As such with manufactured memories, the casualty list includes rationality, reasoning and logical interpretation of events. Memory goes wrong in disastrous ways and the contemporary history bears witness to the same. Memory also is a storehouse of different constituents besides possessing a ready reference for an actual or anticipated event. The past does not correspond to the real in any direct, unmediated way since what we remember are memories-screens always already impressed by the fantasies or distortions of a series of successive remembering. Hence memories, like dreams, are highly condensed symbols of hidden preoccupations.[7]

We must also realise that imagining the past differently from it was can change the way one remembers it. What is it about imagining a counterfactual event that causes people to later become more confident that it really happened? A growing literature shows that imagination can change/alter and even destroy autobiographies and that applies to the persona of all large groups including nation and community.

Memory serves as both a phenomenological position of identity and a carrier for overt identity construction. As memory emerges into consciousness, as it is externalised and increasingly objectified, it depends on cultural vehicles for its expression. In building connections between the past and the present, between who we are and what others perceive us to be, narratives or stories dug from the past have a very important contribution.

One important aspect of memory indicates what people remember. Halbwachs[8] argued, what we choose to remember derives from the social arena, which people always inhabit when they remember. He therefore introduced the term collective memory (memoires collective). Halbwachs[9] stressed how strongly social processes influence not only people's personal memories of their own lifetimes, but also a community's shared memories of the past. Such collective memories are crucial for the identity of groups such as families, believers and followers of a religion, or social classes, James Young should join in here to remind that we should rather speak of collected memory rather than collective memory.

The nature of the networks within a particular place or grouping is of fundamental importance when making judgements about community as a space and community as feeling of solidarity; and the extent to which people can find shared spaces within them. Ability to and availability of opportunities to connect to others and interact with them widens the possibility of a broad spectrum of community. However, shared histories in shared spaces have been one of the most important casualties in the process of othering whereby an adversarial identity is superimposed on them with or without their approval and consent. Perceived superiority and imposed inferiority on to others further complicates community life in locales where familiarity and great social distance can happily go with each other. Identities are capable of creating a deadly web around itself leading to the grounds for destruction for others. It shall not be an exaggeration to underline that people and communities do not always form opinion about the self (us) and others on the basis of their own personal encounters and experiences but largely the guide for interaction comes from above, from distant quarters with or without the consent of the receivers. Such freely rented experiences have added to the make-up and hardened postures of beliefs and a subsequent take on 'self' and 'others'.

Besides, if the local history shared between two communities is adversarial; whether over resources, power or even over memory and history, then the other party is invariably viewed as menacing and threatening to its own survival. Spatial segregation consequently appears as natural adjunct to the politics of dominating space, memory and history. Hence more than the fact that why a community perceived through the conventional wisdom does not exist, it is important is to understand and identify as to how people across the boundaries sustain their everyday engagement amidst rupture. What events, both in the large frame of their lives as occupants of a land experiencing historic changes and in the small frame of their day-to-day world, combine to stir their acts of contentiousness.

Living Together Separately

In the opening lines of his volume 'Community: Seeking Safety in an Insecure World', Zygmunt Bauman (2001) says succinctly- words have meanings: Some words, however, also have a 'feel'. The word 'community' is one of them. It feels good: Whatever the word 'community' may mean, it is good 'to have a community', 'to be in a community'. . . . The meanings and feelings the words convey are not, of course, independent of each other. 'Community' feels good because of the meanings the word 'community' conveys-all of them promising pleasures, and more often than not the kinds of pleasures we would like to experience but seems to miss'.

In fact what Bauman[10] echoes, has been the subterranean feelings behind the use of the term community and has remained to a great extent connected with the anticipation and optimism of reviving the proximate and pleasant relationships which existed in some remote past ages.[11] One of the general tapestries of understanding with regard to the community is that of a social group with a common territorial base and a sense of shared interests and belonging. Shared security, mutual understanding and tolerant outlook plausibly emanate out of this and the profession of social work has never lacked in familiarity with this position at least theoretically. It is not without any substance that the community has been a pivot around which the philosophies governing the human life have revolved and betterment or alteration of the same has also been the innate frames of several ideologies. We reflect on whether there is an unfavourable and visible disconnect of the *reality of community* and community dynamics with the theory and *practice of community* organisation. Going little further on the lines of Nietzsche's *death of God* thesis[12] should we be arriving at *death of community*—even the elusive one!

Overcoming ruptures and breakdown requires addressing causes and symptoms like these more at structural, individual, and intermediate levels. Such holistic approaches are essential for credibility, integrity and building trust amongst communities who have either forgotten the beauty of plural living or have fallen as prey to the *manufactured amnesia*.

References

1. Commission of inquiry set up under the retired Supreme Court Judge M.S. Liberhan to investigate the contexts and the factors that led to the demolition of the Babri Masjid on 6th December, 1992 at the disputed site in Ayodhya (Faizabad).
2. Arendt, Hannah. "*Eichmann in Jerusalem: A Report on the Banality of evil*" in Alexander, 2002.
3. Waller, James. Becoming Evil. Oxford University Press, 2007, p. 12.
4. *Ibid.*, p. 171.
5. Baumam, Z., 2004 *Idenity*, Cambridge: Polity Press, 2004, p. 32.
6. *Ibid.*, p. 38.
7. Halbwachs M. On Colllective Memory. Chicago: University of Chicago Press, 1992.
8. Halbwachs M. On Colllective Memory. London, Harper and Row, 1980.

9. Halbwachs M. On Colllective Memory. Chicago: University of Chicago Press, 1992.
10. Bauman, Z. (2001) Seeking Safety in an insecure world, Cambridge: Polity Press.
11. Hoggett, P. (ed.) (1997) Contested Communities: Experiences, struggles, policies, Bristol: Policy Press, p. 5.
12. Roberts, Tyler T., (1998). Contesting Spirit: Nietzsche, Affirmation, Religion. Princeton: Princeton University Press. Nietzsche seems to be suggesting that the acceptance of the Death of God will also involve the ending of accepted standards of morality and of purpose. Without the former and accepted faith based standards society is threatened by a nihilistic situation where peoples' lives are not particularly constrained by considerations of morality or particularly guided by any faith related sense of purpose.

3

Violence Against Christians: A Case of Study of Anti-Christian Movement in Odisha

Joseph Benjamin[1]

Introduction

Before one tries to study violence against Christians, it would be appropriate to understand the concept of violence. Violence generally signifies an attack or assault resulting in destructive consequence. The Webster dictionary defines violence as an act of extreme force or passion or fierceness. This view construes that the act of violence is primarily physical and focuses on intense emotions that incite violence. However, violence is pervasive. Violence happens everywhere-in street, in public transport, at work place and also at home. No country, city or community is immune or untouched to it. Violence can be perpetrated by strangers, by groups, communities, states, or even people known to victims. Violence is a very complex phenomenon.

Understanding Violence

In common parlance, violence is understood as willful application of such force in such a way that it physically or psychologically injures or causes damage to person, group or property against whom it is applied. Actually the dynamics of violence has long been a preoccupation of the social scientists of all ideological persuasion. Violence is a term that suffers from a surfeit of meanings. Even a cursory glance through the rapidly growing literature on the subject is enough to show the bewildering melody in which the concept is entrapped. The dictionary meaning of violence is the exercise of physical force so as to inflict injury or damage to persons or property. The violence is an act of a person, which encroaches upon the freedom of another. It infringes the rights of other human beings. Margaret has defined violence as the unsanctioned damage to person or property.[1] All violence as such is not condemnable. In fact violence is violence only in the form of and unsanctioned damage to persons or property'. Violence is also man's struggle to adapt to his environment.[2]

According to Random House Dictionary of English Language, "violence means rough or injurious physical force, action or treatment." In other words, it is the expression of aggressive drives on personal and social levels. "Personal violence is a violent act of a man or woman against another man or woman-such as assault and rape, homicide." On the other hand, genocide, concentration camps, communal riots refer to social violence. Some scholars try to relate violence with aggression. Daniels has different view in this regard. Daniels says that 'aggression' is entire spectrum of assertive, intrusive and attacking behaviour. Violence, as a specialised sub-form of aggression, is accompanied by the emotion of anger or hostility; and anger occurs when a plan of action towards a valued goal is interrupted by interference specific enough to warrant attack[3] or "when the expected rewards for attack override other outcomes."[4]

Violence manifests itself in the form of creating law and order situation, beating up people, wrecking cars, breaking into shops and clubs causing extensively senseless damage; indulging in hooliganism; fights among the teenagers and young people; burning of buses and other public property, cinemas, college furniture, etc., youth violence ranges from "eve-teasing" and "goondaism" to rioting, and national and communal violence. Violence can be of different forms.

Encyclopedia of the Social Sciences[5] says that in the social context violence may be defined roughly as the illegal employment of methods of physical coercion for personal or group ends. It is distinct from force or power, which is a purely physical concept.

Genesis of Violence

If one sees the genesis of violence in our ancient society, one can trace it back to the times of Abel and Cain as it is mentioned in the Old Testament Bible of the Christians and Jews. If one sees the meaning of violence, it is the exercise of physical forces so as to inflict injury or damage both spiritual and non-spiritual areas of life. But in the both sense, violence refers to destructiveness. Violence can be considered as the unsanctioned damage to person or property. Ancient time, man glorified in violence and the "man of war" were considered heroes. Attack and win other kingdom was very famous in our Indian history. It is not to be wondered that violence had scriptural sanction. Since scriptures are ancient books of authority, many primordial instincts and customs find a justification in some of these sacred books. Even today the sacrifice of children to god is still prevalent in our Indian society. Sometime in order to please god of rain human beings are scarified.[6] The history of the world shows that violence is a universal phenomenon. It is written large on the pages of human history. Even more paradoxical is the close relationship between violence and human progress as the side effects of war show. The growth of science and technology has not been able to reduce violence but has provided more efficient and more reliable instruments of torture. More the development in science is the more development in violence. Today we have nuclear bombs, which can threaten the humanity of the whole universe. Today more and more missile bombs are manufactured to destroy the humanity.[7]

High level of violence is dangerous to our society. Atomic Bomb and Missiles are disfiguring our society. It is poisoning our most precious institutions, schools and universities and also poisoning the spirit of trust and co-operation that is essential to their proper functioning. Nowadays we are more vulnerable to violence than ever before. A noted socialist, Madhu Dandavate says that social violence has always been the manifestation of certain operation and it inculcates in a society its resultant frustration. For the past few years there have been exploitation of caste, and class tensions.

Violence may be defined as a specific form of force that involves the effort to destroy or injure an object perceived as an actual or potential source of frustration or danger, or as symbol thereof. The present paper would concentrate on the series of communal violences in Odisha. Before studying the violence against Christians, it is pertinent to study communalism, ideological clash and communal violence.

Communalism and Communal Violence in India

Scholars have tried to define communalism in different ways. Some view it as an ideology which emphasises the separate identity of a religious group in relation to other groups and often a tendency to promote of its own interest at their expense. Adherence to a religion or religious system is not communalism. At the same time attachment to any religious community cannot be considered communalism. Indulgence in ritualism, superstition, obscurantism, belief in astrology cannot be a matter of communalism. Communalism means the opposition of religious communities of each other. On the other hand using a religious community against other communities and against the nation is communalism. It is an ideology which emphasises the separate identity of a religious group in relation to other groups and sometime it has a tendency to promote its own interest at their expense. The relationship between two groups becomes hostile, the problem starts and then antagonistic posture of the group itself becomes a substitute for religious and leads to clashes in society.

Once Jawaharlal Nehru, former Prime Minister, had rightly pointed out that the greatest danger for this country is from communalism and not so much from external aggression because when there is external aggression, the people of India tend to get united but when communalism is rampant the people get divided. Communalism is, thus, the most deadly enemy of the people of India.

According to V.R. Mehta, Nationalism and communalism have been the most important factors of the root of major crisis in twentieth century Indian politics. Nationalism has been the aspiration and communalism the disease and both in their ways have shaped Indian Politics.[8]

According to Bipin Chandra, an expert on modern history, "the concept of communalism is based on the belief that religious distinction is the most important and fundamental distinction, and this distinction overrides all other distinctions. Some Hindus, Muslims and Sikhs are different religious entities; their social, economic, cultural and political interests are also dissimilar and divergent. As such the loss of one religious group is the gain of another group and vice-versa. If a particular community seeks to better its social and economic situation, it is doing at the expense of the other."[9]

Communalism and communal violence are two different connotations. In many cases Communal ideology leads to communal violence and riots. Communal ideology is primary and the cause, but communal violence is the consequence. Rioting, looting and killing and other forms of communal violence are contingent or conjectural forms of communal thinking. Communal violence is a consequence of the spread of communal thinking. Communal riot and its cruelty, viciousness, inhumanity, beastliness and barbarity and its toll of many dead and large-scale of destruction of property hits the headlines in Gujarat and Odisha and these have compelled us to study the situations. No doubt communal violence acts as a means of spreading communal ideology. Gujarat violence of February-March 2002 which horrified the entire nation, was the consequence of the prior spread of communal ideology or way of thinking through BJP's and RSS's propaganda machinery, school textbooks, etc., for several years.[10] Similarly, in Odisha, spread of communal ideology led to the communal violence. Here, the communal violence was between Hindus and Christians. On the other hand in Gujarat, the communal violence was between two religious groups, Hindus and Muslims.

Since independence many communal violence has taken place in India. From 1954 to 1963 there were average of 62 communal violence and riots annually and the number of those killed is around 40 per year. Again from 1964 to 1970 the country had an average of 425 communal riots and average of 467 killed each year. From 1971 to 1978 the average number of riots came down 234 and the average number of persons killed to 68. It can be said that the more than 50 per cent of serious cases of communal riots and violence in India are due to inaction, orally ordered by government.

According to the Home Ministry data between 2001 and 2009 6,541 communal clashes occurred and 2,234 persons were killed. Though the number of communal clashes may be correct officially the number of casualties is never reported accurately in official records for various reasons. In 2002 in Gujarat alone, all non-official sources agree, was 2000 dead and official sources are showing number of deaths between 2001 and 2009, i.e., over a period of eight, years as 2,234, i.e., minus Gujarat total number of dead over a period of eight years in all only 234 persons died which can hardly be accurate. But if we take official figure of dead in Gujarat riots of 2002 as 1000, then over a period of eight years 1234 people died, i.e., more than 150 people per year which is not so small, after all.[11] Before studying the communal violence against Christians in Odisha, effort is made to study the concentration of Christians in India in general and Odisha in particular. The communal violence has been continuing every parts of India. Christians are being attacked on the pretext of conversion everywhere. Odisha has been the hot-bed of communal violence. There are number of cases of anti-Christian movement in Odisha. That made us to study the anti-Christian movement in Odisha.

Christians in India

Before one studies the communal attack on Christians, it would be essential to know arrival of minuscule[12] Christian community and their work in India. The history of Christianity in India goes back to a few decades after the birth of Christ, and there is evidence of Syrian Christians having established themselves in Kerala before 100 AD. The Christian presence became more marked in some respects in the nineteenth century after British rule had been consolidated in India, though here again the pretense was often maintained that British rule had no association with Christianity. Even before British rule, Christian Missionaries from Italy, Spain, and Portugal came to India and open schools, dispensary, social work centres. People were influenced and embraced Christianity.

Today, Christianity is a two millennium old religion. It was one of the early eastward movements that first brought Christianity in India. According to tradition it was brought in the first century by one of the apostles of Christ, St. Thomas. This has been the constant tradition of the Syrian Christians of Malabar and it has been widely believed in the West also that this apostle's sphere of work was in India. Since then Christianity is being spread throughout India. Christian missionaries had arrived in India and started schools, social centers, higher educational institutions in India. Through their works they have been influence the people in India. Since then the prosecution started. Many attacks on Christians took place against alleged conversion by Christian missionaries and alleged forced inter-religious marriage. On the pretext of conversion, Christians are being attacked in most parts of India. It is presumed that the number of Christians is going up. But the fact is that the population of Christians is almost stagnant or has been reduced in the sixty years of independence. Despite 1950 years of Christian presence, and around 200 years of British rule the population of Christians in 1961 was 2.44 per cent, in 1971 was 2.60 per cent, in 1981 was 2.44 per cent, in 1991 was 2.32 per cent, in 2001 was 2.34 per cent and in 2011 it became 2.32 per cent. It became clear that the population is almost constant.

It was also said that Christians and Muslim are foreign religions. The anti-Christian violence has been having serious sociological repercussion in small town and villages, especially the places where Adivasis concentration is more. It is alleged that Christian missionary are indulged in conversions which are anti-national. It is also alleged that Christian missionaries are using force and inducement to convert the poor Adivasis into Christianity.

It is important to mention here that India's tyrannical caste structure and exclusionism of the higher castes has been the major cause of the low caste people and Adivasis adopting other religions. The most of the lower castes embraced Buddhism. Buddhism, Jainism and Christianity oppose caste system and that is why many lower castes have embraced these religions. Dr Babasaheb Ambedkar embraced Buddhism in order to get justice within the confines of the traditional Hindu religion. Hindu society prohibits the Shudras from access to public drinking water, entry to temples and also prevented their learning. Similarly many lower castes and Adivasis in order to get social justice embraced Christianity. Many Adivasis in Odisha have embraced Christianity to get away from Hindu traditional fundamentalism.

Asghar Ali Engineer, a noted Muslim scholar points out that conversion could be of four types; (a) conversion through conviction, (b) conversion on account of one's social situation, (c) conversion through inducement and (d) conversion through fraud. The whole history of India bears out that conversion through conviction and fraud are extremely rare. Maximum conversions took place in the history because of social subjugation of lower castes and *Adivasis*.[13]

History of Anti-conversion Laws

Anti-conversion movement is not a recent phenomenon. It has a long history. If conversion is the cause of communal violence in Odisha, then it would be pertinent to study the history of conversion movement in India. Anti-conversion laws date back to the days of British rule in India. However, the earliest laws were enacted by Hindu princes in territories not controlled by the British Empire. The most prominent early laws, namely were the Rajgarh State Conversion Act of 1936 in modern Madhya Pradesh State, the Patna Freedom of Religion Act, 1942, in modern Bihar State, the Sarguja State Apostasy Act of 1945 in today's Chhattisgarh and the Udaipur State Anti-Conversion Act of 1946 in modern Rajasthan. Similar legislation was promulgated in Bikaner, Jodhpur and Kota all in modern Rajasthan State.

After independence, a Congress Party member put forward the "Indian Converts Regulation and Registration Bill" in 1954. This bill required compulsory licensing of missionaries and the registration of converts across India. However, the bill was dropped at the request of then Prime Minister Jawaharlal Nehru. Again in 1960, the Backward Communities (Religion Protection) Bill was presented in Parliament. This bill was also designed to prevent the conversion of Hindus to "non-Indian" faiths on a national scale. However, it was also rejected.

In 1967, Odisha became the first state after independence to enact an anti-conversion law, followed by Madhya Pradesh in 1968 and Arunachal Pradesh in 1978. In 1979, a "Freedom of Religion Bill" seeking official curbs on religious conversion throughout India was introduced in Parliament. The bill was rejected. However, Tamil Nadu enacted a state anti-conversion law in October 2002, followed by Gujarat in March 2003. Tamil Nadu then repealed its law in May 2004, a month after the Bharatiya Janata Party was defeated in national elections.

Anti-conversion laws are currently in force in Arunachal Pradesh, Chhattisgarh, Gujarat, Madhya Pradesh and Odisha. The southern state of Tamil Nadu revoked its anti-conversion law last May after the BJP government was defeated in the 2004 general elections.

The government of Chhattisgarh intends to strengthen the state's anti-conversion law following claims of a rising number of Christian converts. The federal government created Chhattisgarh in November 2000, splitting it from Madhya Pradesh. Chhattisgarh retained the Freedom of Religion Act adopted by Madhya Pradesh in 1968. The Bharatiya Janata Party (BJP), still in control of the state government, believes the existing law is not rigorously enforced and contains too many loopholes.

Under current provisions, a conversion offence is punishable with imprisonment for a maximum of two years, and a maximum fine of Rs 10,000. However if proposed changes were to take effect, "An offence under the law will be non-bailable and punishable by imprisonment of up to four years and a fine up to Rs 1,00,000."

A person wishing to convert will be required to contact district officials 30 days before the conversion. Religious leaders are also required to send a list of would-be converts to district officials 30 days in advance. Officials must approve the conversions before they take place. The new provisions apply only to adults aged 18 years or older and only senior police inspectors are permitted to handle these cases.

Deliberate Needling: Conversion an Issue

The Indian tradition of untouchability lower caste people, are subject to social and economic discrimination. The prejudices remain and 'conversion' out of 'untouchability' has been a push factor for millions of such people to escape from their circumstances through joining other religions. Most of the Panas, tribal groups from Odisha, have converted to Christianity in large numbers and prospered financially. It does not mean that Panas were given money to change their faith. Over the past several decades, most of the Panas have become *Dalit* Christian.[14] Hindu fundamentalist groups have blamed that violence have erupted due to religious conversion. Conversions have been legislated by the provisions of the Freedom of Religion Acts, replicated in some of the states in India. Odisha was the first State of independent India to enact legislation on religious conversions. In Odisha, Freedom of Religion Act, 1967, stipulates that 'no person shall "convert or attempt to convert, either directly or otherwise, any person from one religious faith to another by the use of force or by inducement or by any fraudulent means."' Radical Hindus allege that the Christian missionaries were converting poor tribal people by feeding tribes beef, which is taboo in Hinduism. Also, the missionaries would upgrade the mud houses of the converts into brick-lime. Radical Hindus have further alleged that the increase in the number of Christians in Odisha has been a result of exploitation of illiteracy and impoverishment by the missionaries.[15] The Census of India shows that Christian population in Kandhamal grew from around 43,000 in 1981 to 117950 in 2001.[16]

Violence Against Christians in India

Christians in every State are in minority, except some of the States of the North-East. Now the total population of the Christians is showing some decline. If we take up the case of North India the percentage of the Christians are on decline. The phenomenon is the result of attack on Christian minorities and Churches in India and over all allegations of proselytizing activities. To top it, is the charge that it is a Western religion and aberates the converts from their Indian roots and culture. In this background the Christian minority, meanwhile is virtually helpless to protect them, given tacit approval for these acts of violence by top government officials. "We now see at least one case of violence against every 36 hours somewhere in the country," said John Dayal, a founder of human rights group called "the United Christian Forum for Human Rights". "There were 200 reported cases in 2005 and the real number is much higher", Dayal said many violations go unreported because Christians fear reprisals.

James Massey in his study report[17] tried to show the nature of the violation of minority's rights particularly those of religious freedom. He has cited few cases from 1997 to 1999 where Christian minority was attacked. According to his report there were number of atrocities against this minority. (1) A Christian Priest was attacked and forced to walk naked for eight km, in Dumka, Bihar on 2nd September, 1997; (2) Violation of religious right and police atrocities on Christians in Ludhiana, Punjab on 25th October, 1997; (3) Attack on Minorities (Christians and Muslims) in Gujarat during July and August 1998; (4) Gang rape of four Christian nuns in a village Navapura, Dist. Jhabuva, Madhya Pradesh on 23rd September, 1998; (5) Attack on Christians, and burning and demolishing of Church buildings in district Dangs, Gujarat during Christmas week 1998, (6) The communal violence and attack on Muslim in Surathkal, district Mangalore, December 29–January 6, 1999; (7) Brutal burning to death of a Christian Missionary Graham Stuart Staine and his two sons in Manoharpur, district Koenjhar, Odisha on 22nd January, 1999; (8) Burning of 157 Christian houses in Ranalai Village, district Gajapati, Odisha on March 16, 1999, (9) Burning of Buddhist Monastery in Jaigaon, district Jalpaiguri, West Bangal on 2nd June, 1999. And latest attack on Pastor Walter Masih cannot be ignored. He was attacked by a group of young boys of aged 18-20 in early morning.[18]

National Commission for Minorities member Harcharan Singh Joshi, who conducted an investigation into allegations of harassment of Christians in Madhya Pradesh and Chhattisgarh on Monday, said his probe reveals that administration in the two BJP-ruled States has failed to protect religious rights of the community.[19] "Among the complainants were Bishops of the two States, who were in tears as they spoke about anti-Christian atrocities there," he said.

Even today, Christians are being systematically persecuted across India-with Karnataka leading the list, the All-India Secular Forum and the Catholic-Christian Secular Forum (CSF) alleged in a report on January 12, 2012. Report reveals that persecution has peaked in 2011. It claimed that 2, 141 Christians were attacked in 2011. Attacks are mostly on tribal Christians. Christian missionaries are bringing health and education into villages and Indian hamlets.[20]

Christians in Odisha

Orissa (now known as Odisha) is one of the state of India. It has the population of 3, 68, 04, 660. The literacy rate is 63.08 per cent. The per capita income is Rs 16306. There are 30 districts in Odisha.[21] Followers of Christianity are a small minority in Odisha state of India. According to the 2001 Census, Christians make up about 2.44 per cent of the population (about 898,000 people).

Church of God (Anderson), Council of Baptist Churches in Northern India and Evangelical Missionary Society in Mayurbhanj are among the Protestant denominations of Odisha. Christ Church, the full Gospel Church, Gospel Outreach Ministries, India Evangelistic Association and Odisha Baptist Evangelical Crusade are among the non-Catholic denominations of Odisha working in Odisha. The Church of North India is present in Odisha as well with the dioceses of Cuttack, Phulbani, and Sambalpur. The diocese of Chotanagpur also serves a small part of Odisha. Oraon, Kharia, Pana, Khandha and Munda people are notable ethnic groups with a significant Christian population.

Table-1: Religious composition in Odisha according to the 2001 census

Religion	*Persons*	*Percentage of Persons*	*Males*	*Percentage of males*	*Females*	*Percentage of females*
Hindus	34,726,129	94.35	17,615,951	94.40	17,110,178	94.30
Christians	897,861	2.44	443,245	2.38	454,616	2.51
Muslims	761,985	2.07	391,234	2.10	370,751	2.04
Sikhs	17,492	0.05	9,448	0.05	8,044	0.04
Buddhists	9,863	0.03	5,180	0.03	4,683	0.03
Jains	9,154	0.02	4,736	0.03	4,418	0.02
Others	361,981	0.98	180,156	0.97	181,825	1.00
Religion not stated	20,195	0.05	10,620	0.06	9,575	0.05
Totals	**36,804,660**		**18,660,570**		**18,144,090**	

Roman Catholic Church

Faith came to Odisha more than three centuries ago; but it began to take root in Odisha for the last one and half centuries. Out of 164 catholic dioceses[22] there are five dioceses namely Cuttack-Bhubaneswar, Balasore, Berhampur, Rourkela and Sambalpur and over 500000 Catholics in 37 million people in Odisha. Christian denominations and Catholics together make about one million in Odisha. Total 39 per cent of the people are Scheduled Castes (SC) and Scheduled Tribes (ST).

Attack on Christians in Odisha

There have been series of attacks on Christians in Odisha on the pretext of conversion and reduction of Hindu population. Christians are involved in social activities in Odisha from the very inception of Odisha. Still they are being attacked quite often. It would be appropriate to cite some of the atrocities committed against Christians in Odisha.

Graham Stuart Staines (1941–1999), an Australian Christian missionary who along with his two sons Philip (aged 10) and Timothy (aged 6) were burnt to death by a gang while sleeping in his station wagon at Manoharpur village in Keonjhar district in Odisha, India on January 1999. In 2003, the Hindu activist Dara Singh was convicted of leading the gang that murdered Graham Staines. He had been working in Odisha among the tribal poor and especially with leprosy patients since 1965. Hindu fundamentalist groups allege that he forcefully converted or lured many lower castes into Christianity, however, Staines' widow Gladys Stains denied these allegations. She continued to live in India caring for leprosy patients until 2004 before going back to Australia. In 2005 she was awarded the second highest civilian honor in India, Padma Sree, in recognition for her work with leprosy patients in Odisha.

Another attack on Christians took place in 2007. Though there have been many more attack on Christians, between year 1999 to 2007, they have not been mentioned here. On 24 December, 2007, a group of 150-200 people in the town of Brahmanigaon, in Phulbani district, arrived at the town market and demanded that an arch put across the road by Christians be removed even though the Christian community had received official permission for putting up the structure. The radical Hindu protesters argued that the arch along with a tent set up to organise a Christmas function was sought to be erected on the very site used by the Hindus to celebrate the Durga Puja festival in October. Protestors then sought to close the weekly market and attempted to close all the shops in the area. The Christian shopkeepers refused to comply with this leading to an outbreak of violence.[23] It was not even one month; again Christians were attacked on January 1, 2008. It was reported that at least 20 houses and shops were torched at Phiringia, Khajuripada, Gochapada and Brahmanigaon by rioters on Tuesday night (1st January, 2008).[24] Catholic Bishop's Conferences of India Media centre has made a survey and found the following information about the atrocities against Christians in a short span in Odisha.

Table-2: Destruction and Vandalism and Atrocities against Christians in Odisha (from August 24, 2008 to September 25, 2008).

Houses of Christian families	4063
Churches/Chapels	98
Institutions (Convents, priests' residence, and Training centers)	14
Deceased	38
Displaced persons at Refugee camps	22,236
(Some are in forests and unknown places)	
Total number of displaced persons are between 40,000 to 50,000.	

Background of Khandamal Carnage

Khandamal is deadly beautiful district of Odisha. A tropical forest, but with close mountains and deep valley and a climate that can get alpine in winter, without the snow. The topography of this plateau in the middle of the Indian province of Odisha may have saved the lives of tens of thousands of Christians who fled to the forests as mobs with murder, arson and rape on their minds, attacked 300 villages on August 25, 2008. As reported by John Dayal, state that at the peak of violence around 54,000 men, women and children were hiding in these forests of tall Sal trees where bear and big cats still abound in and trumpet of wild elephants can be heard in the dark of the night. Among those 54, 000 were the families and three dozen Catholic priests twice as many Nuns were hiding and waiting for the moment the police would come to restore order. The Census of India shows that Christian population in Khandamal grew from around 43,000 in 1981 to 117950 in 2001.

The feast of Christmas, an event of joy and peace turned to carnage. The trouble began on 24th December 2007 at 8.00 a.m. at Bamunigam village, close to the police station under Daringabadi Block of Kandhamal District. Kui Kalyan Samiti (a tribal community) had called for a bandh (a means of protest) on 25 and 26 December, Christmas day.(The aim of the bandh was political; it had nothing to do with Christians; but the calling of a bandh on Christmas day was a calculated mischief). Christians suspected trouble. On 22nd December, a Christian delegation had informed the District Magistrate and the Superintendent of Police of Kandhamal district about their fears. The civil authorities promised all help and protection.

As the Christians were preparing themselves for Christmas celebration, some Hindu Fundamentalists forcefully removed Christmas decorations which the Ambedkar Baniko Sangho comprising the local Christian entrepreneurs had put up with due permission from the administration. The Hindu Fundamentalists also stopped the (hatt) weekly market intentionally in order to prevent the Christians from doing Christmas shopping. All of a sudden a crowd of two to three hundred fanatics with destructive weapons began to destroy the shops of Christians. (The Hindu Fundamentalists shopkeepers did not like the shops of Christians which came up in recent years; indeed a challenge to the Hindu fundamentalist shops). They shot at boys. Hearing the gunshots people ran to the jungles to save themselves. All the sixteen Christian shops were looted and torched.

The attackers came in a group of hundreds so that they could simultaneously attack in seven different locations. They broke open the door and looted whatever they could. Then they gathered everything in the middle of the buildings (church, convent, priests' residence, etc.) poured petrol and made a bonfire. Before leaving the place they made sure to smash window glasses, twist the grills and fans. The whole operation was carried out with clinical precision.

According to Archbishop of Cuttack-Bhubaneswer, Raphael Cheenath, SVD said that, "We could not rely on the police or the force." In fact, most of the destruction took place even in the presence of police force. For instance, the church of Bamunigam parish was vandalised and burned in the presence of 20 policemen who just watched.

Quantum of Destruction

As per report of Archbishop of Bhuwaneshwer (CSF reported) the sequence of events is quite clear. The Christian community and its institutions were targeted. The devastation went on for more than 72 hours with the police being physically present on the spot and looking on. The anti-Christian violence continued unabated till 27th December 2007. More than half of 24 parishes in Kandhamal District could not celebrate Midnight Mass because of fear of attack. During Midnight Mass on 24th December, someone threw a bomb at Archbishop' House at Bhubaneswar. It exploded but fortunately no damage took place. Their aim was total destruction of property and weakening of morale of Christian community. There was no attack on clergy and people. During the vandalism that lasted for four days, the following things were destroyed, looted or torched.

Large parish churches	8
Village churches	50 (so far known to us)
Convents	4
Presbytery	5
Hostels	4
Minor Seminaries	2
Vocational Training center	1
Health centres (Balliguda, Pobingia, Srasananda)	3

Source: Archbishop's report from Cuttack-Bhuwaneshwar.

Bogey of Conversion

Christians are accused of 'converting' Hindus to Christianity. Conversion is only a bogy to camouflage their sinister intention of making India a Hindu Nation. Consequently all other minorities should abide by the majority rules; otherwise they are to be ready to leave the country or ready to die. Fanatics are going around in

Kandhamal threatening individuals and families by giving them three options: leave the country, or become a Hindu or be ready to die. The Christians who have witnessed the total destruction of all their belongings feel insecure. The real reason for this calculated atrocities on the *Dalits* (Scheduled Castes and Scheduled Tribes) are the liberation of the *Dalits* whom the upper caste have been treating as 'untouchables' and cheap labour. The church has been in the forefront to initiate a movement in order to liberate them by the dedicated services (education, health, development) of Christian missionaries and NGOs. As a result many of the educated lower caste persons are well-placed in the society and have improved their life in every way. The Upper Caste, who had them under their hegemony all these centuries are now challenged. They are threatened. So, by using the bogey of 'conversion' they want to stop the development of the *Dalits*. They want to protect the hegemony of the upper caste. As they did in the past for many centuries, they want to continue to keep the lower caste under their subjugation, oppressed and marginalised forever.

According to a fact-finding team of the Odisha State chapter of the All India Christian Council, the violence in Kandhamal around Christmas time was perpetrated by radical Hindu groups that killed at least four Christians and burned 730 houses and 95 churches. Hundreds of displaced Christians were in various relief camps set up by the State government.

An incident horrified Christians again. Deelip Mallik s/o Lange Mallick, from a village known as Madinata near Baliguda in Kandhamal district had gone with his family for Christmas-day worship on 24th December. When he returned he found that his house was burnt along with his cows and other domestic animals he reared in a shed attached to his house.[25]

A Ghastly Crime

On 30th September, various news sources reported the case of rape which occurred on 25th August, 2008. The incident took place at K. Nuagaon in Kandhamal district. While a police complaint was lodged soon afterwards, no action was taken for over a month, adding to accusations of police misconduct.[26] Eventually, four men were arrested for the attack, and a senior police officer suspended over the delayed investigation. During a press conference nun said that a group of unidentified persons, dragged her along with Fr Thomas Chellan to the deserted Jana Vikas building. The priest was doused with petrol and beaten up. She reported that the mob paraded her on the streets in the presence of a dozen policemen.[27] After the complaint was launched, a medical examination of the nun was carried out, which showed she had been raped.[28] Police sent the clothes of the said nun to State Forensic Laboratory for further verification. Kandhamal police chief confirmed the rape.[29] Police arrested nine people in connection with the crime, while the nun was in hiding for fear of reprisals. On 22 October 2008, the Supreme court of India, rejected Sister Meena Lalita's appeal for a Central Bureau of Investigation (CBI) probe and asked her to look at an identity parade of those accused to identify the culprit with state police.[30] On 25 October 2008, Sister Meena Lalita appeared before the media for the first time, describing her experience and demanding a CBI probe into the incident. She alleged that the police had been "friendly" with the attackers. She said she went into hiding after the attack to protect herself from Hindutva extremists but decided to come forward after the Supreme Court turned down her initial request for a CBI inquiry.[31]

On 1 September 2008 Government of Odisha claimed the situation was under control. However, 558 houses and 17 churches and prayer halls were burnt in riots. 543 houses were burnt in the worst hit Kandhamal district. 12,539 people were fed in 10 relief camps, 783 people got the facilities in two relief camps in Rayagada district. In all, 12 companies of para-military forces, 24 platoons of Odisha State Armed Police, two sections of Armed Police Reserve forces and two teams of Special Operation Group (SOG) were deployed to control the riots.[32]

Incessant Outrage Against Christians

On December 16, 2011, a Christian has been killed in mysterious circumstances in Kandhamal. Rabindra Parichaa, an activist, who, in the past, has been touring villages and towns in the area, and was from the parish of Our Lady of the Miraculous Medal in Mondasoro in Kandhamal, was murdered. Earlier in the same year, two other

Christian activists, Saul Pradhan and Michael Navak were killed in the area, in Raikia Block.[33] On January 9, 2012 at about 4.30 a.m. Baliguda Police arrested Mr. Junus Pradhan (46), Chairman, Daringbadi Block who is also the President of Christian Jana Kalyan Samaj, Kandhamal. He has been detained at the police station on the false charges of having close association with the Naxal Maoists and is investigating the charges.

Another incident took place same day at about 2 a.m. A group of Police from Raikia police station reached at the house of Pastor Sukadeb Digal (33) at Sipainju (Sipainjari) village, Tiangia, G-Udayagiri Block, Kandhamal district of Odisha and arrested him from his house on false charges of illegal conversion. The police have kept him in Raikia PS up till now and interrogating him while investigating into the matter. He is pastoring over Danekbadi Baptist Church at Daringbadi in which 35 believer families worship together.[34]

Conclusion

Attack on Christians continues in Odisha on the pretext of conversion of tribals. Any form of communal violence, on the pretext of conversion, is to be condemned tooth and nail. There are so many missionaries involved in various services in Odisha. Odisha is considered a bimaru State. Poverty is in its peak. Kalahandi is the example of acute poverty. It can be said that Kalahandi is poorest district of India. Odisha government has established Tribal Ministry. Why governmental scheme does not reach the poor masses and especially tribals? If Christian missionaries are leaving their comfort and start living with poor tribal, what is wrong? If they are trying to educate the tribals, convert their mind-set, don't they think of joining their groups? Even if they embraced Christianity by sheer good work, nobody should consider that a forceful conversion. It is alleged that Christians are using coercion and allurement to convert people. No doubt, forceful conversion is to be condemned. No one should be allowed to convert anyone forcefully. At the same time constitutional provisions are to be respected. Article 25 provides Right to Religion. Under Article 25 all persons are equally entitled to freedom of conscience and right freely to profess, practice and propagate any religion subject to public order, morality and health.

All persons have also been granted the right to establish institutions for religious and charitable purposes manage their own affairs and to own, acquire and administer movable and immovable property. Conversion due to lure can be considered as a grievous sin. It must be condemned tooth and nail. In the end all must say that the good work started by pioneers of church must continue for the well-being of the tribals and not for the sake of conversion. Let's create a violence free state.

References

1. Mahendra Kumar, 1975: Violence and Non-violence in International Relations, Thomson Press (India), p. 46.
2. *Ibid.*, p. 47.
3. D.N. et al. Daniels, 1970: *Violence and the Struggle for Existence,* Little Brown and Company, Boston, 98.
4. *Ibid.*, p. 14.
5. Hook, Sidney, 1935: Violence, *In Encyclopedia of the Social Sciences,* (ed.) Vol. 15, Macmillan Company, New York, p. 264.
6. Narendra Nath Gupta, 1945: *"Side Lights on National Movement in India"* Vol. I. Gandhi and Gandhism Kitabs, Bombay, p. 194.
7. S.P. Aiyar, 1967: *Anatomy of Mass Violence, in the Politics of Mass Violence in India* (ed.) by S.P. Aiyars, Manaktala and Sons, Bombay, pp. 29–30.
8. V.R. Mehta, Ideology, *Modernisation and Politics in India,* Manohar Publishing House, New Delhi 1983, p. 153.
9. Bipin Chandra, *Communalism in India,* People's Publishing House, New Delhi. 1981, p. 2. Also see Bipin Chandra, Communalism A Primer, Anamika Publication, New Delhi, 2004, p. 7.
10. Teesta Setalvad, "How Textbooks teach Prejudice," *Social Action*, October-December, 2000, Vol. 50. No. 4, pp. 384–363.
11. Asghar Ali Engineer, (2011), Social Perspective, Centre for Study of Society and Secularism, Mumbai.

12. As Christians are presumed by majority community. Dr. Joseph Benjamin considers Christian community in India as Voiceless Minority. See, Joseph Benjamin (ed.), "Christians: A Voiceless Minority" New Delhi: Gyan Publishing House, 2006, p. 54.
13. Secular Perspective, Mumbai, January 16, 1999.
14. Sengupta, Somini, Hindu Threat to Christians: Convert or Flee, New York, October 13, 2008.
15. hptt//en.wikipedia.org/wiki/religions_violence_in_Odisha #note-1-16 dated 03/01/2012.
16. Basic Data Sheet District Khandamal, Odisha, Census of India.
17. James Massey, 1999, Rights of minorities to Religious Freedom (A Study Report), National Commission for Minorities, New Delhi, pp. 32-33.
18. *Times of India* (Nagpur edition) April 30, 2007.
19. *Hitavada*, (Nagpur daily) June 20, 2006.
20. *Indian Express* (Nagpur edition), January 12, 2012, p. 3.
21. Manorama Year Book, Kottayam, Kerala, p. 655.
22. *Indian Express* (Nagpur Edition), November 25, 2011, p. 1.
23. Report of the NCM visit to Odisha, 6-8 January 2008, NCM Retrieved on 26/08/2008.
24. Fresh violence in Khandamal, Patil Promises compensation PTI Posted 03/1/2008 Bhuwaneshwar, www.wikipedia.org/wiki/religious_violence_in_Odisha #cite_note_ timesofindia.indiatimes.com-67.
25. CFS reported on dated 29/12/2011, also see, www. thecsf.org.
26. A Nun was raped and Priest brutally assaulted in Khandamal, The Hindu, September 30, 2008.
27. The Time, (London), May 22, 2010.
28. Indian Express, October 3, 2008.
29. BBC News October 3, 2008.
30. www.wikipedia.org/wiki/religious_violence_in_Odisha# cite_note_timesofindia.indiatimes.com-67.

31. www.wikipedia.org/wiki/religious_violence_in_Odisha# cite_note_timesofindia.indiatimes.com-67.
32. www.wikipedia.org/wiki/religious_violence_in_Odisha# cite_note_558houses. 2C_17_places_of_worship. Also *see, Times of India*, September 1, 2008.
33. http://persecutedchurch.info/wp-content/upload/2011/ 12/a_christian_man_looks.
34. CSF news, Mumbai, dated 11/1/2012, www.thecsf.org.

4

Impunity, Fake Encounter and Human Rights in Manipur

Oinam Jitendra Singh[1]

The idea of rights and duties of citizens is as old as the concept of the state. One may find their origin in Ancient Greek political system and in Roman law in Europe, Confucian system of China, the code of Hammurabi, the Islamic political system in the Muslim world and the Panchayat system of India. To have a better understanding of the concept of rights it is essential to look at their history. It can also be said that the idea of rights is as old as human species. As man is a social being and cannot live outside society, the problems of rights arose involving man's relationship with other individuals in a society and his relations with state Governments. Though these relationship men implicitly or explicitly evolved certain norms of social behaviour which got crystallised over century's struggles, into what we call today as Human Rights.

With effect from 26th January 1950, India has adopted a written Constitution. The preamble to this constitution promises to sense to the people of India liberty of thought, expression, belief faith and worship, equality of status and of opportunity and also assure the security of personal life, liberty and dignity of an individual. Part III of this constitution containing the fundamental rights well executes what the preamble promises and assures to the people of India. The Fundamental Human Rights and freedom that are to be enjoyed by an Indian citizen are also found in the ordinary laws-civil and criminal-enacted under this constitution. The Indian constitution was immensely influenced by the Universal Declaration of Human rights 1948. The Apex court in *Kishwanand Bharti V. State of Kerala* (AIR 1973 S.C. 1461 at P. 1510) has observed that the Universal Declaration of Human Rights 1948 though may not be a legal binding Declaration. But it reflects that how founding father of the constitution understood the nature, importance and necessity of Human Rights at the time Indian Constitution was adopted. Even the Judicial Institution and legislative action have been inspired by the Declaration. The Fundamental Rights which is highlighted in the constitution can be enforced by nature.

Manipur has been a controversial part of India since an accord was signed between the King of Manipur and the Government of India on 21st September 1949.[2] Armed opposition groups fighting for the liberation of Manipur from India claim that the accord amounted to annexation. The Government of India has since sent large numbers of troops to Manipur under exclusive military Legislation called Armed Forces (Special powers) Act 1958, itself derived from the Armed forces (Special powers) ordinance of 1942, which was used by the British colonial Government to crack down on the Indian Nationalist movement.

The military authorities impose arbitrary restrictions on civilians, access to their paddy fields, fishing farms and other work places. They conduct military operations without any administration oversight. They make their own rules and enforce them without regard to whether or not they contradict or undermine those of the civil administration, national laws or otherwise. Military personnel also escape independent and impartial justice by having recourse to military tribunals rather than civilian courts. Under the Constitution of India [article 136(2)] offences committed under the Army Act 1950, Air Forces Act 1950 and Navy Act 1957 are excluded from the jurisdiction of the High Courts and the Supreme Court. Similarly the Indian Penal code and Criminal Procedure Code do not give

Criminal Courts jurisdiction over defence personnel in respect to offence committed under these Acts.

The phenomenon of indiscriminate and arbitrary killing by the security forces on the local population continues throughout the years. The Arbitrary killing in the pretext of counter insurgency is not only justified but consider as necessary pattern to tackle the law and order situation in Manipur. This articles attempts to analyse the practice of extra-judicial or extra-legal killing in Manipur by the State security forces within the Human Rights framework, which the government of India has obligation. It is well aware that both the State and non-state actors perpetrate serious form of Human Rights violation by giving their own justification. However, consideration must be given to the distinction between victims of crime and victims of Human Rights Violations. State would treat the violation committed by other than state as crime unless the appropriate legal framework is applied. The Government is yet to recognise such legal framework, which allows the Human Rights and humanitarian agencies to make intervention.

Preference of language is very important to address the issue. The government prefers to recognise the existing situation as mere law and order problems, which is contradicted what the non-State actors prefer to call as national liberation movement. However, Human Rights and humanitarian agencies term such situation as armed conflict. In order to categorise, certain situation as Armed Conflict, defined in International Humanitarian Law, two criteria are usually used: First, the hostilities much reach a minimum level of intensity. This may be the case, for example, when the hostilities are of a collective character or what the government is obliged to use military forces against the insurgents, instead of mere police forces. Second, non-governmental groups involved in the conflict must be considered as "Parties to the Conflict", meaning that they possess organised armed forces. This means for example that these forces have to be under a certain command structure and have the capacity to sustain military operation.[3]

What is an Extra-judicial/Extra-legal Killing?

An extra-judicial killing is the killing of a person by governmental authorities without the sanction of any "Judicial

Proceeding" and "Legal Process"[4]. The term "extra-legal killing" refers to arbitrary deprivation of life such as genocide, war crime, death arising from executions not preceded by proper legal proceedings, death arising from torture or ill-treatment, and death arising from excessive use of force carried out by police, army or other State officials.[5] Therefore, officially claimed "encounter" vis-à-vis *"fake encounter"* as claimed by the other is to be termed as an extra-judicial or extra-legal killing.

India being a part to the International Covenant on Civil and Political Rights (ICCPR) has legal obligation to protect right to life for its citizens under which the protection against arbitrary deprivation of life is *non-derogable* even in a State of Emergency threatening the life of nation.[6] Moreover, the Constitution of India guaranteed right to life under article 21 which stated, "no person shall be deprived of his life or personal liberty except according to procedure established by law."[7] The right to life, which is protected under international and regional human rights treaties, such as the International Covenant on Civil and Political Rights, has been described as "the supreme rights" because without its effective guarantee, all other human rights would be without meaning."[8] The UN Human Rights Committee while considering India's third periodic report under the International Covenant on Civil and Political Rights (ICCPR) in 1997 made the following concluding observation: ". . . . the problems in areas affected by terrorism and armed insurgency are essentially political in character and that the approach to resolving such problems must also, essentially, be political, and emphasises that terrorism should be fought with means that are compatible with the Covenant".

The Committee has also stated: "The Committee regrets that some parts of India have remained subject to declaration as disturbed areas over many years—for example the Armed Forces (Special Powers) Act has been applied throughout Manipur since 1980 and in some areas of that state for much longer-and that, in these areas, the State Party is in effect using emergency powers without resorting to article 4, paragraph 3, of the Covenant. Therefore the Committee recommends that the application of these emergency powers be closely monitored so as to ensure its strict compliance with the provisions of the Covenant."

Article 4 of ICCPR provides that in time of public emergency threatening the life of the nation, the State Parties to the present Covenant may take measures derogating from their obligations under the present Covenant to the extend strictly required by the exigency of the situation.

However, a precondition to avail of this right to derogation is that the State Party should immediately inform the other State Parties to the Covenant, through the intermediary of the Secretary General of the United Nations. It also lists the core rights that cannot be derogated even under an emergency:

Article 6:	Right to Life
Article 7:	Right not to be tortured
Article 8:	Right against Slavery
Article 11:	Right against imprisonment for non-fulfilment of contractual obligation
Article 15:	Right not to hold guilty for an act or omission which did not constitute a crime at the time when it was committed
Article 16:	Right to be recognised a person before the law
Article 18:	Right to freedom of thought, conscience and religion

As pointed out by the UN Human Rights Committee, in the case of Manipur, Government of India have not bothered to make an official proclamation of the existence of a state of emergency but many of the non-derogable rights are routinely violated with legal/official sanction. Extra-judicial killing is rampant. Every village and town of different district in Manipur has similar story of someone get killed or murdered. Official report reveals that more than six thousand people lost their life from 1980 to 2010. Out of which 2106 people had been killed by State Security Forces what they officially termed as "Counter" or "Retaliatory" killing and 2405 people by Non-state actor. A governmental record for the year 1980 to 2010 gives the following statistics corroborates it:[9]

Year	*Total No. of insurgent/underground activist or cadre killed by the both state and Central Security Forces from January 1980 December 2010*	*Total No. of Civilian killed by the insurgent/militant/underground outfit from January, 1980 to December 2010.*	*Total No. of Security personnel killed by the insurgent/ militant/underground organisation from January, 1980 to December 2010*
1980	3	30	20
1981	24	46	19
1982	30	12	48
1983	9	5	3
1984	1	7	15
1985	1	9	47
1986	5	16	22
1987	6	18	24
1988	8	20	31
1989	14	13	27
1990	3	12	29
1991	3	54	64
1992	17	50	33
1993	17	102	31
1994	83	114	91
1995	57	161	61
1996	70	116	63
1997	118	200	113
1998	87	143	65
1999	55	118	63
2000	78	131	52
2001	113	147	30
2002	80	80	52
2003	104	92	26
2004	118	82	35
2005	84	189	47
2006	109	129	29
2007	121	154	41
2008	297	65	13
2009	298	67	19
2010	73	23	5
Total	**2106**	**2405**	**1218**

Fake Encounter in Manipur

There is a high suspicion that maximum of such officially claimed "encounter" or "retaliatory killing" might be fake encounter. Reason would be, in cases of encounter killing or death in custody of the police, certain legal obligations have to be complied. Furthermore, the Supreme Court of India and National Human Rights Commission (NHRC) have given certain guidelines/ directions which are required to be followed.

NHRC guidelines on encounter killing:

1. As soon as information about death being caused in a police encounter is received, the officer-in-charge of a police Station must record it in the appropriate register.
2. It is desirable that the investigation should be handed over to an independent investigation agency such as the Criminal Investigation Department (CID), if members of the encounter party belong to the same police station.
3. Whenever a specific complaint is made against the police for committing a criminal act that amounts to culpable homicide, an FIR should be registered under appropriate sections of the Indian Penal Code and investigation should invariably be handed over to the CID.
4. A magisterial inquiry must invariably be held in all cases where death has occurred in the course of police action. The next of kin of the dead person must invariably be associated with the inquiry.
5. Prompt prosecution and disciplinary action must be initiated against the officers found guilty in the magisterial inquiry police investigation.
6. The question of compensation being given to the dependents of the dead person will depend on the facts and circumstances of each case.
7. No out of turn promotion or instant gallantary rewards will be given to the concerned officers soon after the occurrence. It must be ensured (at all costs) that they are given only after the gallantary of the officer concerned is proven beyond doubt.

8. A six monthly statement of all cases of Deaths in Police action in the State shall be sent by the Directorate General of Police to the NHRC by January 15 and July 15 every Year.

In case of an unnatural death the police is bound to make an inquest report, under Section 174 of Code of Criminal Procedure, 1973 (CrPC) and submit such report to the District Magistrate, Sub-Divisional Magistrate or Executive Magistrate regarding the fact that whether the death of the person has been on an apparent cause or it has occurred unnaturally. But in Manipur most of these inquest reports are filed at the morgue instead of the site where the death has occurred. Thus the filing of the inquest reports fails the object of Section 174 of CrPC as laid down in Sub-Section 1 of the said provision which mandates the police officer to visit the site of the event and investigate. In Podda Narayana-V-State of A.P. [AIR 1975 SC 1252, (1957) Cr LJ 1062] the object of the inquest report is laid down by the Supreme Court of India are:

1. To ascertain whether the person died under suspicious circumstance.
2. To determine the cause of death.

Inquest report can be used under Section 145 of Indian Evidence Act although; it cannot be used as substantive evidence during trial. Thus, when inquest report are filed at the morgue the nature of death cannot be established properly resulting in failure of the police duties which raises serious question in encounter killing.

In case of death under police custody, the judicial inquiry should be made by the Judicial Magistrate under Section 176 (1) of the CrPC. However, "inquiries regarding extra judicial execution are conducted by an Executive Magistrate rather than a Judicial Magistrate, violating Section 176 of the Criminal Procedure Code (Amended 2005). Executive Magistrate have limited knowledge of law and are not mandate to make judicial opinions."[10] Furthermore, the Malimath Committee Report has recommended that a separate Prosecution Department should be formed under Home Ministry to look into affairs of the police. NHRC with its letter No. 66/SG/NHRC/93 to the Chief Secretaries of all States and union Territories dated 14 December, 1993 clearly directed the concerned District Magistrate and Superintendent of Police is to report every custodial death/encounter killing to the Secretary General of the Commission within 24 hours. The Commission has even cautioned that the failure to report promptly would give rise to presumption that there was an attempt to suppress the incident. However, State Government has failed to comply such direction. According to NHRC, 111 cases have been report as police encounter case. Therefore, Chief Secretary, State of Manipur shall explain as to why the report are not being forwarded to the National Human Rights Commission"[11] But in practice, the police and other law agencies give different notion regarding the video filming of the post mortem procedure for custodial death/encounter Killing is presumed to be sought permission from concerned Executive Magistrate as a require legal step".[12] Even the access of post mortem report (which can be the biggest suggestive aids in order to establish valuable evidence) is denied to the victim's family.

Moreover, almost all encounter Killings carries similar story that the victim got killed in encounter or retaliatory fire either. However, the family members of victim or people who witnessed the incident very often refuted such official version claiming the victim to be either innocent or arrested/abducted from some other places. In some cases, the families claimed the victim to have carried bundle of cash and found out the victim attiring unmatched combat dress, with clear signed of Torture mark.

It is also quite usual that the responsible security official who leads the encounter file report to the Office-in-Charge (OC) under whose jurisdiction the incident has taken place. Based on Such report, the concerned OC registered an FIR accusing the deceased to be members of proscribed organisations. In almost all cases, the police do not record any FIR on behalf of the victim's family. The usual justification that the police have given is that an FIR which has already been registered may initiate the investigation. However, such investigation never happened as the investigations are closed as the case having abated, in view of the death of the accused. The police also sometimes tell the victim's family that prior permission of Judicial Magistrate is required to lodge their complaint. The table on the next page may tell what would be the truth[13]:

Year	*Killed in officially claimed "encounter" or retaliatory fire or "Cross fire"*	*Refutation by family members/witnesses as Killed after arrest/abduction*	*Family members claimed the deceased to be innocent/ civilian/labour/government employee/teacher/contractor*
2011	9	4	1
2010	73	11	1
2009	298	43	34
2008	297	50	51
2007	121	15	12
2006	109	11	19

People's suspicion on encounter killing is increased as the particular citation of gallantry award, an award entitled to those security personnel who did the extraordinary job has never made disclose at public. NHRC's guidelines also clearly stated that "no out of turn promotion or instant gallantry rewards will be given to the concerned officers soon after the occurrence. It must be ensured that they are given only after the gallantry of the officer concerned is proven beyond doubt".[14]

The families and the human rights organisations have tried every door of the institutions of democracy starting from the local police station to the Chief Minister's office to institution a judicial inquiry against the perpetrators. But, in most of the time the authority have been responded with empty promises. Thus, such behaviour of the law enforcing agencies and the government raise questions regarding the encounter death.

Conclusion

The people who are the victims of extra judicial killings are from the villages of different part of Manipur. Almost all the victims belong to lower middle class and extremely poor family. In rare circumstances, middle class became a victim of encounter as the result of personal enmity or quarrelling with security personnel. Most of the victims are observed to be sole bread earners for the families. Thus, by killing one person extra-judicially, the security forces have been able to paralyze the whole family economically. More than the racial prejudices, which is often the basis of suspicion for the security personnel; the act of such seems to be a systematic breakdown of the economic support of the families.

"Extra-judicial executions in Manipur, mostly young men, resulted in the proliferation of young widows and orphans. The widows face the double burden of being a young widow in a traditional patriarchal society as well as the stigma of being branded as families of terrorist.[15] Families of encounter victims are not entitled to schemes or facilities initiated by the Government. Their children also face social stigma as they grow up with the humiliation and disownment from the society as the kin of terrorists throughout their lives.

"The need to collectivise and bring together the widows and mothers to combat the continuous extra-judicial executions has created the formation of Extrajudicial Victims' Families Association, Manipur (EVFAM). The spirit and objective of the forum is to use domestic as well as international redressal mechanism to seek justice and to rehabilitate the widows and their children."[16] Extrajudicial Execution and human rights can never go together on the same side. Till and until the term Extrajudicial Execution refers, there would be always violation of human rights. The cause of Extrajudicial Execution may be of reasonable for the perpetrator, but the acts of Extrajudicial Execution always remain as inhuman.

References

1. Faculty, Centre for Human Rights and Duties Education, Manipur University, India.
2. *Article* 2. Vol. 5, No. 5, Asian Human Rights commission, December, 2006.
3. Christopher Harland "*Basic documents on International Humanitarian Law-South Asia Collection (Treaties, National Legislation, Case Law and Other Documents)*" p. 796.
4. *http://en.wikipedia.org/wiki/Extrajudicial_Killing#Extrajudi cial _Killing_Summit*
5. High Commissioner for Human Rights, Centre for Human Rights, *Professional Training Series No. 5, Human Rights and Law Enforcement (A Manual on Human Rights Training for the police)*, United Nations, New York and Geneva, 1997, p. 88.
6. Article 4 and 6 of ICCPR.
7. Chapter III, Article 21 of Constitution of India.

8. Office of the United Nations High Commissioner for Human Rights, *Terrorism and Counter terrorism (fact Sheet No. 32)* p. 8.
9. Obtained under Right to Information from Ministry of Home Affairs, Govt. of India (No. 8/9/2011-NE.I dated 22 Sept 2011) and Home Dept. Govt. of Manipur (No. 14/4(69)/2010-H (RTI).
10. Joint Stakeholders Report, India Status of Human Rights in Manipur (North East Region) Submitted to the Office of the High Commissioner for Human Rights, 2nd Cycle Universal Periodic Review, Human Rights Council, United Nations by Civil Society Coalition on Human Rights in Manipur and the UN. p. 6.
11. NHRC letter No. 22/14/2004-2005-DB-II/FC dated 28th January 2010.
12. NHRC letter No. NHRC/ID/PM/96/57 dated 27 March 1997 to Chief Ministers of States.
13. Human Rights Alert, Manipur, India, 2011.
14. NHRC's revised guidelines/procedures to be followed in dealing with deaths occurring in encounter deaths.
15. *Joint Stakeholders Report*, No. 8, p. 7.
16. Human Rights Alert "*Human Rights Diary* 2009".

5

Challenges to Free and Fair Elections in the Hills of Manipur: A Study of the ADC Elections 2010

S. Mangi Singh

Introduction

Free and fair elections are one of the most essential pre-requisites for any democratic political system. It facilitates meaningful representation of the people in matters of governance, and lends credence to freedom of political expression, freedom of speech, freedom of choice, etc. which are available to the people of a country. The danger which the absence of it poses to democracy is only too evident to one and all. If the process of electoral politics is not conducted in a free and fair manner, no elections however grand their scales might have been or however regularly they might have been held, won't amount to much in terms of securing popular basis and legitimacy for the political system. Because it is not so much the election result figures but the actual process of electoral politics through which those results were arrived at that will decide the democratic content or otherwise of an election. Keeping this in view, when one looks at the trend of electoral politics in the hills of Manipur, one cannot help but observe the increasing pressure on the conduct of free and fair elections in the Naga dominated areas there. This has become a very serious concern in times of local, state as well as national elections. The subject matter of the paper is being located in the context of these considerations with the hypothesis that free and fair election is becoming more of a myth than a reality in the Naga dominated areas of the hills of Manipur.

Autonomous District Councils in Manipur

The Autonomous District Councils (ADCs) in Manipur were inaugurated for the first time in Manipur in the year 1973. These ADCs were established under the then existing Manipur (Hill Areas District Council) Act, 1971. These six ADCs are established in the hills of the state namely; (1) Chandel Autonomous District Council; (2) Churachandpur Autonomous District Council; (3) Sadar Autonomous District Council; (4) Senapati Autonomous District council; (5) Tamenglong Autonomous District council and (6) Ukhrul Autonomous District Council. The 2010 ADC elections marked the fourth time that the District Councils in the state went to polls. It was also the first time since the passing of the Manipur (Hill Areas) District Councils (Third Amendment) Act, 2008 and it was under the provisions of this Act that the ADC Elections 2010 were held. It may also be noted here that prior to the 2008 Act, the Act of 1971 was amended twice,—the first in 1975 and the second in 2006. In between, the Manipur Legislative Assembly also had enacted the Manipur Hill Areas Autonomous District Councils Act, 2000 which provided for the repeal of the Act of 1971. However, the Act of 2000 was never brought into force.[1]

The 2010 ADC Election Contests and Results

The ADC elections for the six autonomous District Councils were held in two phases—the first on 26 May and the second on 2 June 2010. Of the six ADCs, Churachandpur, Chandel and Sadar Councils went to poll in the first phase while Ukhrul, Tamenglong and Senapati Councils went to poll in the second phase. There were altogether 144 Autonomous District Council Constituencies (ADCCs) in the six ADCs, with 24 in each of the ADCs. Out of these, 69 candidates were elected uncontested which include 9 from Churachandpur, 12 from Sadar, 12 from Chandel, 20 from Ukhrul, 12 from Senapati and 4 from Tamenglong District Councils.[2] In the remaining 75 ADCCs there were no candidates in 8 ADCCs, six in Senapati and two in Ukhrul. As such, polling was scheduled only in 67 ADCCs. These were 15 in Churachandpur, 12 in Sadar Hills, 12 in Chandel, six in Senapati, two in Ukhrul and 20 in Tamenglong. Again, out of these 67, there was no voting turn out at all in two ADCCs (both in Senapati ADC) as the candidates in these ADCCs announced their retirement from the elections after their candidature were duly accepted by the election authorities.[3]

Once the results of the elections in the 134 ADCCs were out (this is without the eight ADCCs where there were no candidates and the two ADCCs where there was no voting turn out at all due to the retirement of the candidates), it was clear that the Congress won a landslide victory in the elections. It won a total of 106 seats out of a total of 144 with the Independents winning 25.[4] It was a success story for the party from the word go with 68 of its candidates (32 during the first phase and 36 during the second phase) winning the elections uncontested. About the remaining seats, the CPI won one, the Trinamool Congress won one and the NCP won one.[5]

Dissenting Notes on the Eve of the Elections and Pressure Against the Conduct of Free and Fair Elections

Dissenting notes whenever an election is about to be held and undue interference from different quarters putting all sorts of pressure on the conduct of free and fair elections have become a norm in the hills of Manipur. This will be true for national, state and local level of elections. Still, the extent to which these things happened in the context of the ADC Elections last year has been most disheartening. One may start with the dissenting notes first. As soon as the government announced its intention to hold the elections, there was an upsurge of dissenting notes from the Nagas and their organisations inside the state. For instance, the United Naga Council (UNC) strongly opposed the elections to the ADC under the Manipur (Hill Areas) District Councils (3rd Amendment Act) Act 2008.[6] It asked all the Naga candidates to withdraw their candidature by giving them 48 hr time stating that they filed their nominations against the decision of the Council taken in a series of consultative meetings of the Naga frontal organisations held at Ukhrul, Taphou, Tadubi, Kangsang, Chandel and Tamenglong.[7] Reiterating that the meetings unanimously rejected the 2008 Act, the UNC further warned that those who refuse to withdraw their candidature shall be treated as anti-people and anti-national and that the Council will not be responsible for the dire consequences on account of non-compliance.[8]

The Tangkhul Naga Frontal Organisation (Against ADC Election 2010) called for a 72 hr total bandh in Ukhrul District from the midnight of 31 May to oppose the ADC elections.[9] The Organisation in its meeting with the Council of Tangkhul Headmen, Chairmen and Hangva (Village Council) decided to support the United Naga Council's (UNC) decision to boycott the elections. Criticizing the state government for neglecting the aspirations and voice of the people, it appealed to all voters concerned and the citizens to adhere to the UNC's decision and abstain from casting votes, and participation in the election.[10] It even warned that any untoward incident arising due to non-compliance of the resolution will be the sole responsibility of the individuals concerned.[11] There was also the UNC's call to boycott the elections condemning the 2008 Act as against the interests of the hill people. The All Naga Students' Association (ANSAM) also imposed an economic blockade on the national highways passing through the state demanding the deferment of the election.[12] Likewise, the Zeliangrong Students' Union also imposed a bandh in Tamenglong district from the midnight of 28 May to the midnight of 2 June.[13] Senapati District was also under the grip of a 48 hours bandh starting from the midnight of 31 May.[14] It was called by the Senapati Students' Association. The elections in Chandel District were also held amidst a 48 hours bandh called by Naga civil societies.[15]

It may also be noted that due to pressure from various quarters including important Naga Civil society groups, seven MLAs from Naga dominated constituencies even submitted their resignation to the Speaker in support of the move to boycott the ADC elections.[16] It is altogether a different thing that all these seven have been members of the Hill Areas Committee of the state Legislative Assembly which supported the ADC Act.

Apart from these dissenting notes, there were also the outright pressure put on both candidates and voters to boycott the elections. For instance, one Congress candidate (Paojalet Touthang) contesting from Chingdai ADC constituency of Senapati district was abducted by unknown persons. He was later released in the evening of the same day.[17] Another Congress candidate (S. Benthung Anal) who contested from the 13-Vomku ADC constituency was also kidnapped by miscreants from his native village.[18] Reports of many candidates receiving threats, telling them to withdraw their candidature and that otherwise they will face dire consequences were also there. There was also the deadline of May 17 for the withdrawal of their candidature set forth by the UNC. In fact, following all these developments and also on the request of the candidates, the state government had to arrange secure shelters for them at the SAI Youth Hostel and State Youth Centre at Khuman Lampak Sport Complex where personnel of the 2nd IRB guarding round the clock. About a total of 50 to 60 candidates were expected to stay at the SAI Youth Hostel while another 40-50 candidates were expected to stay in the State Youth Centre.[19] At one time there were altogether 85 candidates taking shelter in these two places.[20] Of these five were from Chandel, 26 were from Senapati District, 24 including two women were from Ukhrul District and the rest were from Tamenglong District. Of these four districts, Ukhrul and Tamenglong are Naga dominated districts whereas the in the other two both constitute more or less two equally effective communities and even from these two districts also, it is mainly from the Naga dominated ADC constituencies that the candidates came to take shelter. The Commanding Officer of the 2nd IRB was made responsible for the security of the candidates by detailing armed personnel at the two buildings. In addition, the SPs of the Imphal east and west districts were also asked to provide additional security to the candidates in addition to the security personnel already detailed at the two hostels.[21]

There were also many reports of attacks on the residences of the candidates who refused to comply with the ultimatum of the UNC. Houses of many candidates in Ukhrul district were attacked.[22] The house of one Congress candidate RK James who had been declared elected uncontested from the Phuba ADCC in Senapati District was also dismantled by miscreants in the wee hour between 12 a.m. to 1 am of 31 May.[23] There were also reports of another candidate's house and a school meant to be a polling station set on fire by unidentified elements in Senapati District.[24] A group of people who came to vandalize the house a candidate in Noney, Tamenglong District was also driven away by the local womenfolk.[25] The house of one Congress candidate S. Mohring was also set on fire by some unidentified miscreants at Chandel District Headquarters.[26] All these instances in one way or other may be regarded as acts to sabotage or acts to thwart meaningful participation of the people in the electoral politics concerning the ADC elections. Attempts were also made on the National Highways to block the poll personnel from reaching their polling stations. For instance, officials for 33 polling stations and security forces guarding them were reportedly unable to reach their assigned places due to the disturbances created by the NSCN (IM) cadres and their supporters who had caused damages to the roads and bridges the poll personnel were supposed to pass through.[27] In fact three vehicles carrying polling personnel heading to Tamei for poll duty were pushed down the gorge and smashed by supporters of the election boycott call. They even stoned and smashed the windshields of around ten vehicles belonging to the IRB personnel accompanying the poll personnel to protect them.[28]

Interacting with one of the local dailies at a 'safe house' in the capital, the candidates for Ukhrul ADC expressed remorse that the Tangkhul frontal organisations have taken such a harsh stand. Noting that the ADC election has come after many years, the candidates also explained that the election process began at the recommendation of the Hill Areas Committee of Manipur Legislative Assembly which comprise all the tribal MLAs of the state.[29] One of the candidates regretted that if the Naga frontal organisations wanted them to block the conduct of the elections, instead of asking them to withdraw their candidature, then they should have done before they have sought political patronage from political parties and filed their nominations. Another candidate also expressed that if these organisations were against these elections then they should have castigated the tribal MLAs in the Hill Areas Committee instead of targeting them.[30] The candidates also pointed out that the ADC elections have not been held for about 22 years prior the proposed 2010 elections and that such a delay in constituting the ADCs has deprived the hill people of the state the benefits of many welfare programs taken up by the government. They believed that the formation of the ADCs will better facilitate the involvement of the people at the grass root level in time of the implementation of numerous development programs in the hill areas. They also expressed their apprehension that such an opposition to the ADC elections will create dissensions among the Naga communities.[31]

It may also be noted that the other prominent Naga insurgent organisation-NSCN (K), came out strongly against the efforts to obstruct the smooth holding of the ADC elections. It urged all concerned to ensure a free and fair election to the ADC as well as to participate in the election.[32] Describing them as some "purported" civil society organisations, it criticised the United Naga Council, the Naga People's organisation and the All Naga Students' Association Manipur for deliberately misleading the people. The NSCN (K) also said that these organisations have caused unnecessary confusions and have spread all sorts of misconceptions and fallacies leading the people of the whole Nagaland to descend into total chaos.[33]

All these developments created an atmosphere of uncertainty, tension and fear for the candidates as well as the voters in and around the time of the conduct of elections, particularly in areas where the Nagas inhabited and where the Nagas and Kuki-Chin-Mizo group of people co-existed. It is evident from the fact that out of 60 polling stations in Chandel District where both the Nagas and Kuki-Chin-Mizo group of people constitute two more or less equally effective communities, the ratio of normal, sensitive and hyper-sensitive polling stations was 3:45:12.[34] According to the District Election Commissioner in the District, most of the voters were prevented from the exercise of their franchise right.[35] There were reports of voters not coming out of the polling stations even after casting their votes due to fear of what may happen to them; agents inside the polling station refusing to be photographed by the press again for the same reason; voters telling the press that they did not cast their votes as they were warned not to cast their votes; many voters standing outside their polling stations fearing to enter and entering to cast their votes only after the arrival of security personnel; etc., were also there.[36]

What happened in the Naga inhabited areas was quite in contrast to what one saw in the Kuki dominated areas. For instance, the Kuki National Organisation (KNO) announced three regulations for the smooth functioning of the Autonomous District Council elections in the state to ensure public peace and orderly atmosphere. Hailing the initiative of the government to hold the elections after a gap of about two decades as an attempt to strengthen local self government in the hills of the state, the KNO issued a strict and mandatory compliance order for all to ensure and facilitate the passage of the true spirit of democracy in the state.[37] It also prohibited any form of canvassing of votes by using threats and intimidations or in an unruly manner in the name of any organisation. Saying that booth capturing shall be dealt with seriously, the KNO also appealed to all the voters to exercise their voting right freely and without fear.[38] Then it comes as no surprise that overall, the voting turn out in the Kuki dominated areas was considerably higher than in the Naga dominated areas with Churachandpur and Sadar Hills recording 90 per cent and 75 per cent voting turn out respectively. Compare to it, the voting turn out in Chandel, a district where both Naga and Kuki-Chin-Mizo group of people constitute two more or less equally effective communities there recorded 48.3 per cent only.[39]

About Senapati, Tamenglong and Ukhrul, out of the 24 ADCCs each in all these three Naga dominated ADCs, there were elections in only six ADCs in Senapati, only two in Ukhrul and 20 in Tamenglong. Again, 20 candidates from Ukhrul, 12 from Senapati and four from Tamenglong got elected uncontested. Besides, the eight ADCCs where there were no nomination at all (six in Senapati and two in Ukhrul) and the two where there were absolutely no voting turn out due to retirement of candidates from politics (both in Senapati) were also in the Naga dominated areas. This means, there were actual electoral contests in only 28 ADCCs out of the 72 ADCCs in these three Naga dominated ADCs.

Concluding Remarks

The experience of the ADC elections 2010 in the hills of Manipur clearly shows that free and fair elections have become more of a myth than realty in the Naga dominated areas of the hills of Manipur. The trend has greatly endangered the prospects of growth of healthy democratic traditions in the hills of Manipur. What happened in case of the ADC elections 2010 was not an isolated one. Rather it is continuation of a trend that had emerged much earlier. It was there during the 12th, 13th, 14th and 15th Lok Sabha elections and in connection with the 9th state Assembly elections which took place in 2007. This has resulted in the decline of electoral politics conducted on the basis of part competition in many parts of the state. Compared to this, the trend in the valley is one of electoral politics conducted on lines of party competition. Constraints on the conduct of free and fair election is much less there because of less interference or dissenting notes from both civil society groups and insurgent organisations. If the current trend in the hills continues, which I fear is not likely to stop in any near foreseeable future, it will seriously endanger the prospects of realising there those democratic traditions and practices which the country wants to realise under the provisions of our democratic constitution.

References

1. H.L. Shangreiso: Repeal Manipur (Hill Areas) District Council Act, 1971, Nagaland Post, online edition, http://www.zogamonline.com/articles/atangpi/3965-repeal-manipur-hill-areas-district-council-act-1971.html accessed on 4.12.10.
2. Hueiyen lanpao, an English daily, Imphal, 23.6.2010, p. 1.
3. *Ibid.*
4. The Sangai Express, an English daily, Imphal, 22.6.2010, p. 1.
5. *Ibid.*
6. UNC Warns on ADC Polls, Hueiyen Lanpao, 10.5.10, p. 1.
7. *Ibid.*
8. *Ibid.*
9. 72 hr total bandh in Ukhrul District from May 31, Hueiyen Lanpao, p. 1.
10. *Ibid.*
11. *Ibid.*
12. Despite open threats ... ADC candidates refuse to budge, The Sangai Express, 20.5.10, p. 1.

13. 2nd Phase ADC Polls: Bandh and Blockade Stop Poll Officials, The Sangai Express, 30.5.10, p. 1.
14. *Ibid.*
15. All Set for First Phase Poll in Three Hill Districts, Hueiyen Lanpao, 25.5.10.
16. *Ibid.*
17. The Sangai Express, an English daily, Imphal, 11.5.10, p. 1.
18. Hueiyen lanpao, an English daily, Imphal, 19.5.10, p. 1.
19. Hueiyen Lanpao, an English local daily, 17.5.10, p.1.
20. *Ibid.*, 19.5.10, p. 1
21. *Ibid.*, 17.5.10, p. 1.
22. Houses of nine ADC candidates ransacked, http://e-pao.net/GP.asp?src=5..010610.jun10, accessed on 26.11.10.
23. Hueiyen Lanpao, 2.6.10, p. 1.
24. http://www.e-pao.net/epRelatedNews.asp?heading=11&src=020610, accessed on 26.11.10.
25. *Ibid.*
26. The Sangai Express, 28.5.10, p. 1.
27. Hueiyen Lanpao, 2.6.10, p. 1.
28. *Ibid.*
29. The Sangai Express, 21.5.10, p. 1
30. *Ibid.*
31. *Ibid.*
32. The Sangai Express, 26.5.10, p. 1.
33. *Ibid.*
34. *Ibid.*, 27.5.10, p. 1.
35. *Ibid.*
36. *Ibid.*
37. Statement issued by Th. Stephen Kuki, Under Secretary, Publicity and Information, KNO, Churachandpur, dated 24.5.10.
38. *Ibid.*
39. Mixed bag in turn with Churachandpur recording 90%, The Sangai Express, 27.5.10, p. 1.

6

Understanding Adivasis Violence

Gladson Dungdung

Introduction

Adivasi literally means aboriginal, original settler or first settler of the land. Indian Constitution has classified *Adivasis* as the Scheduled Tribes (ST) and guaranteed certain rights and privileges. According to the census 2011, the Adivasis are 8.6 per cent of the total population in India. Out of this around 11.3 per cent tribals live in rural areas whereas 2.8 per cent live in urban areas. About 85 per cent of them live in Rajasthan, Gujarat, Maharashtra, Madhya Pradesh, Chhatisgarh, Odisha, Jharkhand and West Bengal. About 12 per cent live in North east states like Assam, Arunachal Pradesh, Nagaland, Meghalaya, Manipur and Tripura (Sopan. Down to Earth; July 31, 2003).

Population of Scheduled Tribes in Different States of India Census 2011

Top 5 States/UTs		*Bottom 5 States/UTs*	
Lakshadwep	94.8%	Uttar Pradesh	0.6%
Mizorum	94.4%	Tamil Nadu	1.1%

Nagaland	86.5%	Bihar	1.3%
Meghalaya	86.1%	Kerala	1.5%
Arunachal Pradesh	68.8%	Utarakhand	2.9%

The *Adivasis* live in or around the forests and their life cycle moves around nature. They do not only depend on natural resources for their livelihood, but their culture, identity and autonomy are also based on it. Ninety per cent of them still live in or in close proximity to the forests (Pradeep. 2004) and only 10 per cent of them have shifted to the cities. That's why some call them *vanwasi*.

Basically, the Adivasis are known for autonomy, peace, justice, collectives and honesty. However, in the 21st century, they are the worst sufferers of violence, either inflicted by the state agencies or non-state actors like the Maoists. In both the cases the human rights of the Adivasis are violated. The matter for the biggest concern is that a number of Adivasi youth have taken up the guns after being influenced by some ultra-left groups. Therefore, this paper examines why a peace-loving community has adopted the path of violence. Why do youth see the gun as panacea for their problems? Why did the Indian State fail to contain the discontents? What went wrong with the Indian democracy after 67 years of Independence which put the community on the path of Violence? Why have the guns become a part of life for the villagers in the mineral-rich corridor?

Historical Background

In ancient times, the Adivasis had ownership rights on natural resources and they judiciously used these resources for their survival. Consequently, the Adivasis were living with autonomy, peace and prosperity. The situation changed after the Aryan invasion and became worse during the British rule. On the one hand, the Aryans destroyed the Adivasi civilisation, denied the indigenous identity and did not accept them as fellow human beings, and on the other the Britishers used violence on the Adivasis by grabbing their land, territory and resources and even named few of them as criminal.

Soon after the East India Company arrived in India, the Britishers realised the enormous commercial potential of India's natural resources and systematically went about acquiring control over the land, territory and resources by capturing power, introducing legislations and using military. In response to the British Indian government, the Adivasis revolted against them. This is how violence entered into the Adivasi community. Adivasis used their traditional weapons against the Britishers.

In 1779, the Adi`.si legend Baba Tilika Manjhi dared to challenge the Britishers by saying, "Our people have lived here since the dawn of creation. We have never been the lords of the earth. The earth is our mother. We are all her children. We are the trustees of this land. It is our responsibility to see that the land continues to sustain future generations that we have not even imagined. This is our heritage. Then how can you, British, an alien race, declare yourselves the lords and masters of the forests that sustain us and give us life? How can you deny us entrance to the only home we have ever known? We will die before we accept this rule." (Dungdung, 2004).

Perhaps, Baba Tilka Manjhi was the first Adivasi leader who led an organised struggle against the British in 1779. The Britishers surrounded the Tilapore forest from where he was operating the fight but he and his men held the enemy at bay for several weeks. When he was finally caught in 1784, he was tied to the tail of a horse and dragged all the way to the collector's residence at Bhgalpur. There, his lacerated body was hung in a Banyan tree (http.wesanthals.tripod.com). However, in 1793, the Britishers imposed the "Permanent Settlement Act" on the people to get more revenue from land, which affected the socio-economic and cultural lives of the Adivasis, and their lands slipped into the hand of the Zamindars (landlords). Thus, the community ownership on land was overthrown by the Zamindari System.

'The British introduced a centrally organised administration, a judiciary and a police system. The concept of private property was imposed on land as opposed to the traditional notion of collective usufructuary rights of the community. The community resources were considered as the 'eminent domain' and taken over. Thus forests and other individually unclaimed fallow lands were declared as the property of the state' (Munda & Mullick, 2003). Gradually, the government enacted various forest policies, which induced the marginalisation of the Adivasis. They were deprived from the natural resource merely for the government's revenue-yielding measures. Imposing revenue on land and duties on the forest produces crashed the "Adivasi economy". The Britishers also brought the Land Acquisition Act in 1894, which helped them to strengthen their rule by destroying local people's rights over natural resources. Later the Act was amended in 1984.

After India's independence the status quo remains. The painful reality is that so far as the monopoly over natural resources is concerned the Indian rulers were not different from the Britishers. 'The vested interest, the methods of oppression and the basic ideology remain the same' (Anjum & Manthan, 2002:4). The Adivasi rights over the natural resources were snatched away through various legislations. As a result, the Adivasis' discontent, anger and resistance manifested day by day. The government of India accepts through the Forest Rights Act 2006 that the historical injustice was done on the Adivasi community but it did not bring appropriate mechanism to right the wrong instead the whole community was labelled as 'Naxalites' and accused of waging war against the Indian State. A very interesting point to note is that a few Adivasis used violence to protect their land, territory and resources whereas the Britishers and other Indians (non-Adivasis) adopted violence for capturing the land, territory and resources of the *Adivasis*.

Captured Forests

After taking control of the land, the Britishers' eye went on the forests. In 1855, the British Indian government declared the forests as government property; therefore the individual cannot have right and claim over it. The Santal Hul (Revolution) of 1855 was an organised community response to the Britishers' resource grab. However, the Britishers continued their job of snatching community resources by various ways and means. In 1865 the first Forest Act was enforced, an avalanche of regulations followed this act. Wherever a loophole was detected in the existing laws a new law would be passed. The Forest Act, 1927 enabled the government to take over any piece of land after declaring it as forest land.

The Government of India constantly strengthened its control over the forests by enacting numerous policies in the name of protection, preservation and conservation of forests and wildlife. The people's access to forests and de-reservation of the reserved forests was completely ceased by the 'Forest Conservation Act 1980' and access to forests was also denied to the community by the

Wildlife Protection Act 1972. After hue and cry, the Government introduced a new policy in 1988, which is called the 'National Forest Policy 1988'. It advocates the protection of rights of Adivasis and concessions to them. But it was seldom practiced.

The 21st century witnessed the worst atrocities on *Adivasis* by the State. The Government of India issued an order following the Supreme Court's verdict in 2002 to evict the illegal encroachments on the forests and forest land. The *Adivasis* were depicted as encroachers of the forests in the government's order. The order also describes the encroachment of forests by powerful lobbies. But ironically 'none of the powerful lobbies, the letter alludes to, was touched; nothing was done about the front line staff of the forest department who did not take timely action against the encroachments by powerful lobbies but the *Adivasis* were the first target and though the exact numbers are not available, the number is close to 25,000 evictions (Prabhu, 2004).

The forest policies deprived Adivasis of their livelihood resources and also depicted them as encroachers and enemy of the forests and wildlife. At the same time, the policies have dis-articulated the social, economic and political systems of the Adivasi community. On the one hand, Adivasis have been deprived of the right to life, health and education, and the sponsored development and social security schemes of the Government are also denied to them. These are denied merely because they live in the (reserve) forests, which fall under the ineligible category, according to Government rules.

However, the Indian State brought the Forest Rights Act in 2006 to right the historic wrong but its implementation is dubious. On the one hand, the implementation of the Act is extremely poor and Adivasi lands are still being handed over to the corporate houses for the so-called development projects, and on the other, the forest department, which is the biggest landlord on earth, doesn't allow Adivasis to enjoy their rights and privileges on forests.

Land Alienation

The Adivasis consider land as heritage. The Adivasi legends Baba Tilika Manjhi, Sidhu-Kanhu, Birsa Munda and many others considered land as their mother and heritage. They fought against the British to protect their lands. However, the Adivasis were alienated from their heritage by those so-called civilised masses who consider the land merely as property. The state of Jharkhand is one of the best examples to understand the Adivasis' land alienation.

The land alienation had begun during the medieval period but it arose rapidly during the British regime. The British introduced "Zamindari System" by enforcing the 'Permanent Settlement Act' in 1793, which created upheavals in the Adivasi community. Consequently, a series of Adivasi upsurge took place in the region-the Santhal uprising in Santhal Parganan (1855), Kolh revolution (1831) in Kolhan and Birsa Ulgulan (1895) in Chotanagpur, which resulted in enforcement of three legislations—Chotanagpur Tenancy Act 1908, Wilkinson's Rules 1837 and Santhal Pargana Tenancy Act 1949. The prime objectives of these legislations were protection of Adivasi land, traditional self-governance and preservation of culture. But these laws were seriously violated.

In 1969, the Bihar Scheduled Areas Regulation Act was enforced for prevention and legalisation of illegal land transfer of Adivasis. A special Area Regulation Court was established and the Deputy Commissioner was given special right regarding the sale and transfer of Adivasi land. According to the provision, an Adivasi cannot sale or transfer land to another Adivasi without permission of the Deputy Commissioner. When the special court started functioning, a huge number of cases were registered. According to the Government report, 60,464 cases regarding 85,777.22 acres of illegal transfer of land were registered till 2001-2002. Out of these 34,608 cases of 46,797.36 acres of land were considered for hearing and rest 25,856 cases related to 38,979.86 acres of land were dismissed.

After the hearings, merely 21,445 cases regarding 29,829.7 acres of land were given possession to the original holders and the rest remains with the non-Adivasis. Furthermore, 2,608 cases of illegal land transfer were registered in 2003-2004, 2,657 cases in 2004-2005 and 3,230 cases in 2005-2006, which clearly indicate that the cases of illegal land transfers and the resultant land alienation are increasing rapidly. According to the Annual Report 2004-2005 of the Ministry of Rural Development of the Government of India, Jharkhand topped the list of Adivasi land alienation in India with 86,291 cases involving 10,48,93 acres of land.

A prominent Adivasi leader and Vice-Chairperson of the National Commission for SC & ST, Bandi Oraon, had undertaken a study on the implementation of various legislative measures meant to protect illegal transfer of Adivasi lands to non-Adivasis in the State. The study was confined to 15,703 cases registered in the Ranchi Collectorate in respect of Adivasis living in and around Ranchi City. The study reveals that merely 41.46 per cent cases were accepted for hearing, 26.82 per cent cases were rejected and 31.72 per cent cases were kept pending. But interestingly, out of the total hearings, actual possessions were given in 96 per cent cases.

The non-Adivasis have used many tricks for acquiring lands possessed by Adivasis. The best way of buying Adivasi land is to marry an Adivasi girl and register the land in her name. This trick was widely used by the non-Adivasis. Secondly, many Adivasis surrendered their land to the money lenders after being trapped by them through loan. Besides, threatening, coercion and illegally prepared documents were also used for acquiring land. Authorising the Deputy Commissioner for land transfer also caused huge loss to the Adivasis as many non-Adivasi officers justified land transfer to non-Adivasis. In many cases, the court also defined the laws in favour of non-Adivasis.

Another major fact is that the Chotanagpur Tenancy (CNT) Act was amended in 1947 for the purpose of urbanisation, industrialisation and for development projects which caused land alienation on a huge scale. Finally, the land-related laws were utterly misused, violated and mis- interpreted against the Adivasis by the policy makers, bureaucrats and other non-Adivasis.

Displacement

The stories of tribal deprivation are unending sagas. Approximately 50 million people were displaced in different projects from 1951 to 1995 in the name of development in India. The bitter fact is that around 40 per cent of them belong to the Adivasi community. More than 15 million hectares of land was acquired all over India. 'As per government records, at least 75 per cent of those displaced are still not cared for or rehabilitated' yet (Fernandes & Paranjpye, 1997: 6).

Adivasis were discriminated against in receiving compensation. For instance, NALCO built two units in Odisha in mid 1980s. One of them was in Koraput district, which has a tribal majority and the other in Angul, which was pre-dominated by upper castes. About 58 per cent of all land acquired is in the form of Common Property Resources (CPR). Displaced people of Koraput received a compensation of Rs 2,700 per acre, while those of Angul received Rs. 25,000 per acre. Most tribals who hesitantly parted with their lands by giving in to NALCO, 20 years ago, reside in small huts with naked, shabby children and scantily clothed women around the huts.

In the state of Jharkhand, around 17,10,787 people were displaced while acquiring 24,15,698 acres of lands for setting up power plants, irrigation projects, mining companies, steel industries and other development projects in Jharkhand. In every project, approximately 80 to 90 per cent Adivasis and local people were displaced but merely 25 per cent of them were rehabilitated half-heartedly and no one has any idea about the rest 75 per cent displaced people. The benefits of these development projects were highly enjoyed by the landlords, project officers, engineers, contractors, bureaucrats, politicians and outsiders, and those who sacrificed everything for the sake of the "development" are struggling for their survival. The people were betrayed in the name of rehabilitation, compensation and jobs. The promises were not fulfilled and the jobs were given to outsiders. However, the forced land acquisitions are still going on across the country.

The Indian State amended the Land Acquisition Act in 1984 and brought a legislation for the corporate houses called Special Economic Zone (SEZ) in 2005 but did not bother to make a law for the rehabilitation of the displaced masses. The proposed Rehabilitation and Resettlement Bill 2007, which seems as an improvement on the existing Land Acquisition Act, has lapsed and now has to be introduced afresh in the Lok Sabha. Similarly, when Jharkhand state was created, its first Chief Minister, Babulal Marandi introduced a new industrial policy, but at the same time, the Government was unable to enact a rehabilitation policy.

It is obvious that 'the Indian state has been far more concerned with promoting corporate interests in tribal areas than in enforcing their rights and entitlements' (Iyer, 2010). This is why the intention of the state was always questioned and the people are resisting displacement everywhere. The people were displaced from one place to another but they were not rehabilitated. They feel cheated and wronged by the State-in the name of "development" and "national interest". Therefore, now the Adivasis believe that they can protect their land only through mass struggles.

Denial of Identity, Language and Culture

Adivasis have been dwelling in India approximately 3,500 years before the Aryan invasion and they are the original inhabitants of the country, also called Indigenous People. However, the Indian State constantly denied them this status. In 1993, Mr. Jayant Prasad, a Government of India representative, clearly stated in front of the UN Working Group on Indigenous Population in Geneva that there is no such Indigenous People existing in India. The Indian state doesn't recognise the Adivasis as the Indigenous People of the land. Instead, they are labelled as forest dwellers. The Britishers classified them as Scheduled Tribe, which was adopted in the Indian Constitution, too.

The word 'Adivasi' can hardly be found in any of the official documents across the country. According to a prominent educationist of Jharkhand, Dr. Nirmal Minj, the Adivasi word was not accepted by the Indian society. Therefore, it is not used in any official document although the Adivasis feel proud of being called 'Adivasi'. Adivasis do not come under the *Varna System* of Hindu society but very sad that they are asked to produce the caste certificate while going for higher education, government services and welfare schemes.

The Constitution recognised many regional languages and adopted those as the official languages of several states but the languages spoken by the Adivasis, many of which have scripts and used in day-to-day life, were completely neglected. However, a few Adivasi languages like Santali, Bodo, etc., were incorporated in the eighth schedule of Indian Constitution only in 2003. Adivasis had played a major role in the freedom struggle. In fact, Adivasis were the first people who fought against the Britishers but they were not accorded the due space in the Indian history.

The culture that Adivasis practice is very unique and derives its strength from natural resources. The close relationship of Adivasis with nature, their unique culture and ethos are manifested on their wall paintings, life style, relationships, attitudes and behaviour. The folk songs, dance, music, paintings, male and female dancing together in social events are the most significant expressions of their culture. It clearly shows their collective living, thinking, unity, equality, autonomy and freedom of expression they practice. To a large extent, the Adivasi women enjoy much more freedom and equality when compared with the women of the so-called mainstream society.

Adivasis have their own traditional methods, techniques and wisdom of imparting social and cultural knowledge to their children and educating them about different spheres of life. The Adivasi children learn all the cultural activities, expressions and community livings from their parents, which help them to grow in an independent atmosphere. 'Such a culture has been basic to their survival, which is built around the natural resources. Through the centuries they have developed such a conservative culture that has helped them to view their life support system as a community resource inherited from their ancestors, to be used judiciously and preserved for posterity. In other words, their traditional culture is community-based. It has equity and conservation of the resource i.e., sustainable development and use of the resource as its basic principles (Fernandes, 2002). They have varieties of festivals, such as, Makar Parab, Baha Parab, Sarhul, Karma, Jitiya, Sohrai and so on. There has been a deliberate attempt on the part of the Indian State to deny, neglect and destroy their identity, language and culture.

Destruction of Socio-economic and Political System

Based on collectivism, equality, autonomy, non-profit ethos and indigenous democracy, the Adivasi society is very close to the nature. They are endowed with rich and glorious historical, cultural and political heritage. The basic human values, which are the essence of a primary human society like simplicity, truthfulness, respect for elders, caring and sharing, co-operation, communitarian life styles, subsistence economy, human spirituality, collectivism, etc., are still visible in their society.

The political system of the Adivasi society is based on autonomy, self-rule and self-determination, which is also known as the Adivasi self-governance system. Consensus is the principle of this system, where there is no space for bad politics, monopoly and money. While the Britishers were clever to recognise these traits of the Adivasi political system, the Indian State has deliberately been neglecting them. The Indian State forcefully imposed electoral politics on the Adivasi community. The Panchayati Raj Extension in Schedule Areas Act 1996 also known, as PESA, is the best example to understand how the Indian State destroyed the best practices of indigenous democracy through imposed elections.

The Adivasi communities depend on agriculture and forest for their sustenance. They mostly practice agriculture, collect minor forest produce to meet their everyday needs and also rear livestock to sustain their economy. An Adivasi family collects only that much of food grains and minor forest produce which it needs for a year and the rest is left out for other families. However, the Adivasi economy was crashed by the market economy of the so-called "civilised world". The market economy which is actually the war economy, creates competition among the communities, intensifies individual greed and war among the communities. The social, economic and political systems of Adivasi communities were destroyed and other systems were imposed on them.

Conclusion

Adivasis are the Indigenous People of India, who have a unique culture, identity and autonomy. However, the Indian State did not recognise their indigenous status, neglected them in terms of development and denied those rights and justice. Adivasis do not only depend on natural resources for their livelihood but their entire social, economic and political systems, including identity, autonomy and distinct culture are based on natural resources. They are not only consumers of the natural resources but also protectors and conservators of the same. They have their century-old comprehensive methods, rules and policies for preservation, protection and conservation of the forests.

The Adivasi territory is being called today as the "red corridor". Adivasis are accused of waging war against the Indian State. But the fact of the matter is that Adivasis did not adopt the path of violence by choice or pleasure. They have been driven to the wall. The State has grabbed their livelihood resources through various policies, laws and with the use of force. They were not only neglected in terms of development but are also described as people who oppose development. Their identity, culture, autonomy, and self-rule have been destroyed. They are labelled as separatists, anti-national and enemy of the Indian State. They have been socially discriminated against economically exploited and dispossessed from their resources. Corruption in politics and bureaucracy always impeded development in the Adivasi regions. Police atrocities on Adivasis continue unabated. Consequently, they feel most vulnerable and have lost their hope in the Indian democratic system. Therefore, some of them have adopted the path of violence to counter the state violence.

However, the Indian State sees only two ways-development and military action as panacea to end violence. Ironically, the same government, which accepts doing historical injustices to the Adivasis through the Forest Rights Act 2006, doesn't talk of justice, peace and prosperity. The issue of violence cannot be countered only through development approach and military action precisely, because the injustice, discrimination and denial are the foundation of violence. The government must address the problem in a holistic manner. That includes political security, development, justice and end of discriminatory policies, protection of distinct Adivasi identity, culture and ethos, and public perception of management fronts as well.

References

Areeparampil, Mathew. 1995. Tribals of Jharkhand: Victims of Development. New Delhi: Indian Social Institute.

Anjum, Arvind and Manthan. 2002. Displacement and Rehabilitation. Pune: NCAS.

Ahmad, Nesar. 2003. Women, Mining and Displacement. New Delhi: Indian Social Institute.

A. Tejaswini and K. Ashsish. 2000. Joint Protected Area Management. Pune: Kalpavriksh.

Bijoy, C.R. 2004. Lesson from Muthanga, pp. 25-27.

Bakshi, P.M. 2002. The Constitution of India. New Delhi: ULP.

Das, Vishya. 1992. Conservation, Government and Tribal people.

Economic and Political Weekly (Mumbai) March, p. 567.

—1998. A State against its people. Economic and Political Weekly (Mumbai) Dec., pp. 30-31.

Desai, Basant. 1991. Forest Management in India. New Delhi: HPGH.

Das, N.K. (Compiled) 2003. The Odisha Forest Manual. Cuttack: OLR.

Das, Susanta. 2004. Odisha Forest Act, 1972. Cuttack: OLR.

Dungdung, Gladson. 2003. Life for Livelihood. Indian Currents (New Delhi) June.

—2003. Sowing Seeds of Hatred in Adivasis' land IC (New Delhi) August 17.

—2004. Forest Rights. Indian Currents (New Delhi), April 11.

Fernandes, Walter (ed.) 1992. National development and tribal deprivation. New Delhi: Indian Social Institute.

—1993. The indigenous question: search for dignity. New Delhi: Indian Social Institute.

— (ed.)1996. Drafting a people's Forest Bill. New Delhi: Indian Social Institute.

Madhav G. and Ramchandra G.1995. Ecology and Equity. New Delhi: Penguin.

Heramath, S.R. Kanwalli, S. and Kulkarni, S. (ed.) 1994. All about draft Forest Bill and forest land. Bangalore: SPS.

Heramath, S.R. (ed.) 1997. Forest lands and Forest produce. Bangalore: NCPNR.

Iyer, Manishanker. 2010. Missing the woods, the trees. New Delhi. *Hindustan Times,* May 20.

Joshi, Sopan. 2003. Defunct Democracy. Down to Earth. (Mumbai) July 31.

K. Govind and Nathan Dev. 1991. Gender and Tribe. New Delhi: Kali for Women.

Krishna Kumar, R. 2003. A conflict in the forest. Frontline (Chennai) March.

Louis, Prakash. 2000. Marginalisation of Tribals. Economic and Political Weekly (Mumbai) Nov. 18.

Lobo, Brain. 2004. Unequal access to justice. Combat Law(Mumbai) December-January.

Munda, R.D. and Mullick, S.B. 2003. The Jharkhand Movement. New Delhi: IWGIA and BIRSA.

Prabhu, Pradeep. 2002. Tribal face genocide. Combat Law (Mumbai) Oct. 2004. Tribal interface-logic of survival. CL (M) December-January.

Pathak, Neema and 2001. Tribal self-rule and natural resource management.

Gour, Vivek., New Delhi: Kalpavriksh and IIED.

Rajagopal, P.V., 2002. Voice of hope, voice for change. Pune: NCAS.

Ramagundam, Rahul. 2001. Defeated Innocence. New Delhi: Grassroots India.

Samuel, John. (ed.) 2002. Struggle for Survival. Pune: NCAS.

—1998. Triple burden. Humanscape (Mumbai) December, pp. 12-13.

Sharma, B.D., 2003. Forest Lands. New Delhi. Sahyog Pustak Kutir Trust.

Saberwal, Vasant. Rangarajan, Mahesh and Kothari, Ashish. 2000. People, Parks and Wildlife. New Delhi: Orient Lognman.

Thundiyl, Jacob (Com.) 2002. Creating Voice for Indigenous People. Chennai: NACDIP.

Thapar, Romesh. 1977. Tribe caste and religion in India. New Delhi: Macmillan India Ltd.

N.A. N.D. The Santhals. New Delhi: AISWACS.

N.A. 2003. Report of the first national conference. Nagpur: NFFPFW. N.A. N.D. In defence of their forest. A report of Malkangiri Adivasi Movement published by Rangaraja Kanma (Hyderabad).

N.A. 2002. Land for life: promise and performance of land reforms in Madhya Pradesh. Pune: NCAS.

Yorke, Micheal and Rao, J. 1977. Tribes of India. New Delhi: Oxford University Press.

7

Terrorism: Anatomy and Prevention

Mohan S. Kashikar

Introduction

Terrorism has become a global menace today and has attracted the attention of the entire world particularly after the attack on WTC on September 11, 2001. India is the country which has suffered the most due to this menace. This greatest challenge to the humanity in the 21st century has its roots in the 20th century. In the following pages attempt has been made to understand the definition, characteristics and development of 'Terrorism'; India's case and her response to it; its global face and possible solutions to tackle this menace.

Definition

Terrorism is . . .

- a form of politically motivated action combining psychological (fear-inducing) and physical (violent action) components carried out by individuals or small groups with the aim of inducing or compelling the state or the authorities to meet their demands.

- the use of violence by a group acting either on behalf of, or in opposition to, an established political authority.

Characteristics

1. First and most important key element of terrorism is the intention to terrorise or create terror in the minds of people;
2. Terrorists always resort to extra-ordinary violence, something unusual, something unprecedented, unbelievable, which will create fear-psychosis in the minds of the people;
3. So, it is natural that all the terrorist acts involve use of weapons of all types;
4. The immediate victim of terrorist is just symbolic rather than instrumental;
5. Their target is always civilian, because common men can "be easily compelled to do things by the fear of death or injury or pain which they otherwise would not do;"
6. The action is carried out in such a way that it will attract maximum publicity;
7. The real target is much bigger and wider or the effect sought by terrorist acts is much greater than the actual physical damage;
8. The acts are meticulously planned and deftly executed;
9. The acts involve very little or no investment, but the result, impact or outcome is far wide, far great;
10. There are men (members of the terrorist organisation) who are indoctrinated by the ideology (necessarily religious), who are even ready to die for the cause. These men are possessed by the divinely ordained philosophy that it is their fundamental, sacred duty to die for the 'highest cause';
11. These possessed men are influenced by what may be called the divine philosophy of death, which promises them that their souls will directly enter the heaven by virtue of their supreme sacrifice;
12. Terrorist acts are usually followed by an explicit demand or there may be a hidden massage. Demands are of varied types:

(a) release of prisoners from the jail;
(b) demand for a special fund for development of an area or a group of people;
(c) demand for separate statehood;
(d) demand to secede from the country and creation of a separate nation.

13. There may be an implicit threat or a hidden message to the other party to mind its own business, to concede the longstanding demands as early as possible or a warning not to interfere in cultural, social, political or religious affairs of the group or organisation or even the state;
14. Lastly, the terrorist group as such is numerically very small and therefore they do not dare to launch direct and open offensive against their enemy. So the terrorism is the instrument in the hands of cowards.

All these characteristics can be seen in any of the Terrorist Acts that have taken place all over the world so far. Whether it is terrorism in Israel, Palestine, Cuba, Syria, Egypt, Iran, Iraq and Chechnya; which attack on WTC or whether the acts of terrorism in Punjab, Kashmir, North-eastern states of India or the attack on Indian Parliament or Mumbai. Attack on Mumbai prima facie looks like a heroic attempt by some spirited individuals.

Anatomy and Modus-operendi of the Terrorist Group

The anatomy or organisational structure and modus operendi of the terrorist group is very secret, but a general picture can be drawn about it. The group is woven around a leader, either a religious leader or a political figure, called the 'supreme commander' or 'commander-in-chief'. This leader never comes out in open nor meets anybody from the group except his close associates. The leader is surrounded by a group of very close associates or confidants called 'the coterie' or core group. This group is directly in touch with the leader and is well conversant with his plans, ideas and vision. These groups and leaders are always travelling or keep on changing their hideouts. The second line-up includes 'commanders' who operate in different areas or are given specific duties. They always report to some leader in the core group, but never the C-in-C. They are assigned the task of establishing contacts with the 'second line-up of commanders' and the 'common followers', propagate the ideology of the group, arrange for purchase of arms and ammunitions, arrange all types of training camps for the new recruits, collect funds for the group and coordinate terrorist activities in their assigned area. There may be a second line-up of junior commanders if the area of operation is widespread or the size of the group is very big. This group is also assigned the similar task like the higher group. The last or lowest layer of terrorist group consists of a 'periphery' called the followers or sympathisers. They are scattered all over. They act as messengers or spies. They do petty jobs like transporting goods and food items, giving shelter to the terrorists, etc. They also mingle with the people, bureaucracy and keep track of the political leaders. They provide crucial information to higher-ups on the basis of which terrorist actions are planned. Most of the people from the periphery work for the group out of fear. But some of them may rise above in the organisational hierarchy after successful indoctrination and rigorous tests of skills and loyalty. Indoctrination is done through the video and audio tapes of speeches of the leader, through publications highlighting the ideology of the group and the injustice and atrocities committed on to the group, by constantly flaring up racial and religious sentiments and continuous hammering out the feeling of superiority and sacred nature of the group.

Since the terrorists believe in the cult of violence, their modus operendi is in tune with their philosophy. Besides killing people at gun-point the terrorists resort to many other acts like, exploding bombs at public places; high-jacking planes, buses and trains; abducting important personalities, leaders and so on. They are very innovative in devising novel methods as can be seen from the human bomb that killed Rajiv Gandhi and attack on WTC or Mumbai. The terrorists are silent killers. They choose the target, time and technique. The whole act is done very swiftly within remarkable time. The other party is caught unawares and before they could react the terrorists complete the job.

Philosophy of Terrorism is basically rooted in the extreme ideologies like Nazism and a deep urge to establish superiority of a country or a race or a religion or a political ideology. This has been a game in international politics. In 1930's, Hitler devised and used techniques of torture, suppression, blackmailing and all types of brutalities to wipe out the opponents in Germany. Communist regimes in the Soviet Union and China and other dictatorial regimes in many European, African and Asian countries used the same techniques to annihilate their opponents within their respective countries. This was known as state terrorism. International manifestation and wider application of the same techniques and philosophy was experienced during the cold war period after the Second World War. The two super powers gave all types of help to their friendly countries in order to wipe out the people of opposite ideology and consolidate the puppet regimes there. This financial and military help was diverted to create groups that indulged in proxy wars and all sorts of terrorist acts in the enemy country with the objective to destabilise that country. Thus, there emerged many terrorist groups in West Asia particularly. In the 1980's, the US gave aid to create a counter-force against the communist forces and their puppet regime in Afghanistan. Pakistan capitalised on this by quickly siding with the US and with its help Taliban was created. The same Taliban has now boomranged against the US and terrorist groups like Al-Qaida have become the enemy No.1 not only of USA but the entire humanity.

Thus, the terrorism has crossed national boundaries of the state and has become its latest *avtar* called International Terrorism. Today, terrorists are helped, openly or secretly, by one state against the other. Their task is further made easy by the extensive use of modern technology like computers, satellite links, cellular phones and latest and highly destructive weapons. This has enhanced the organisational skills and destructive capacity of the terrorists. However, this has complicated the task of the civilised world to counter this menace.

Second ugly face taken by the terrorism is its association with religious fundamentalism, particularly with Islamic fundamentalism. This association also began during 1980's when the US with the help of CIA launched a policy to throw out Soviet forces from Afghanistan. Pakistan jumped into the picture with its ISI trying to give it a *Jihadi* colour of a war of all Muslim world against the Soviets. Tens of thousands of Muslims joined the *Jihadi* training camps on Pak-Afghan border. In these US-sponsored camps military guerilla training was integrated with the preaching of Islam. Thus, there was a combined force of CIA, ISI, Taliban and *Al-Qaida* during 1980's acting against the Soviet Union. Even after Soviet withdrawal from Afghanistan, Taliban in association with the ISI of Pakistan, Wahhabi sect of Saudi Arabia and Mujahidin mercenaries continued to operate in Central Asian Republics of former USSR. These forces continued their support to newly independent Central Asian Republics and civil wars in Kosovo, Chechnya, Bosnia and Macedonia. Taliban established its full control over Afghanistan and soon issued dictates on the lines of the Shariat. The US turned its blind eye to all inhuman activities of the Taliban. The breakdown of Soviet Union left a vacuum in world politics and without any formidable challenge the US started acting like a super-cop of the world. The economic wealth of the US, its military strength, its open social order, its value system and its aggressive foreign policy in the post-cold war period resulted in a kind of resentment in the rest of the world. The developing countries particularly expressed their resentment openly. But the opposition from the Muslim world was more vocal, open and direct as can be seen in the aggressive postures of President Mahathir. The reaction of Taliban perhaps was strongest one. It turned out that the wealth and strength of the US became a highest factor of repugnance for Talibanis who were languishing in poverty, were still respecting age-old value systems and were greatly inspired by Islamic laws. This gradually turned Taliban against the US, who had to face an unprecedented incidence of attacks on WTC and the Pentagon. This tragic incidence has almost divided the world into two camps, Islamic and non-Islamic and brought the world on the verge of third world war.

Third factor associated with the terrorism is the trade of narcotic drugs and smuggling of weapons. Traditionally, territory of Pakistan and Afghanistan is known for the production of opium. In 1980's this region became world's top producer of opium and heroin. The CIA ignored and sacrificed this drug war to fight the main objective of cold war. With the disintegration of Soviet Union, the Central Asian Republics, Afghanistan and Pakistan formed 'the Golden Crescent Drug Triangle'. The CIA and powerful business syndicates in CAS tried to control the drug trade. This trade financed the terrorist activities. The well-established intelligence network of ISI in this region came handy in this trade. Secret sale of weapons also became a flourishing allied business of the terrorist network. There were agents and middlemen who supplied second generation arms to the terrorists. The lobby of arms factories in the developed countries was most eager to do this kind of business. Some rogue countries also participated in this business.

Thus, terrorism has become a highly complex issue as a result of combination of all these factors.

Terrorist Activities in India

Terrorist activities in India began in the late 1960s in the form of Naxalite movement. It was a group of radical leftists inspired by the experiments in China under Mao. This group was active in Andhra, Bihar and Kerala where petty land-lords, money-lenders and government officer were killed. But the movement soon lost its grip after the death of their leaders.

In 1956, there was a movement for independent state of Nagaland, but it became weak after the leader escaped to England and its movement died completely in 1963 when state of Nagaland was created. In Manipur, the Meitei gave a call for abandonment of Hinduism and return to the century-old Meitei faith. Thus, there started a crusade against foreigners or non-Meitei.

In Tripura also the militant tribals started a movement against non-tribals. Creation of separate states of Mizoram and Meghalaya resolved the problem of Mizos, but some hostile elements are still active there. Assam was gripped by terrorism in the 1980s when the students started a movement against the foreigners who had migrated from the neighbouring Bangladesh. Later the Bodo community also demanded a separate statehood on the basis of different race and religion.

Terrorism in Punjab was the most serious problem in the 1980s. Few Militant Akalis demanded a separate and sovereign state of Khalistan on the grounds that Sikhism is a different religion altogether signifying different culture and philosophy. They denied the inclusion Sikhs in the definition of Hindus in the Article 25 of the constitution. The leaders of this movement were operating from abroad, but large number of militants had made the Golden Temple their hideout. The militants were flushed out using a policy of bullet for bullet. Militants took revenge by assassinating our prime minister. But with strong and persistent policies by the govt. together with positive developmental schemes, terrorism in Punjab was curbed successfully and peace returned to the state within a decade.

Terrorism in Kashmir is by far the greatest challenge before India. Militants there are banking upon the support of Pakistan and China and have rejected accession of Jammu and Kashmir to India. They also take advantage of the initial mistakes committed by Indian leaders. They raise the demand for referendum to ascertain the wishes of the people. The issue was unnecessarily taken to the UN which resolved to maintain the status-quo. India has fought three wars with Pakistan over Jammu and Kashmir and 3rd of Kashmir is in Pakistan's possession. It has been proved beyond doubt by Indian and American intelligence agencies that Pakistan is actively supporting terrorists in Jammu and Kashmir. The issue has become very complicated now.

So, it is clear that India has been waging a war against terrorism for the last 25 years. Her concerns, her views were never taken seriously until 9/11. When India pleaded with the US about the proxy war in Jammu and Kashmir, it kept on pontificating to us to the need of peace talk. Now as the US itself is hurt by terrorist, it is taking revenge. But still it is asking us to keep restraint and negotiate with Pakistan, who continues to give active support to the terrorist in Jammu and Kashmir. World opinion has definitely turned in India's favour and India is getting wide support over her stand on Jammu and Kashmir and terrorism. Pakistan which once helped US to raise these terrorists now is leading partner of US, because only Pakistan knows the ground realities and geographical conditions in Afghanistan. Pakistan played all its diplomatic cards very effectively to gain twin benefits; one, to create an image of herself as a secular, modern, civilised nation and; two, to dig out as much aid as possible from the US for its dwindling economy. The rulers of Pakistan, whether politically elected or a military dictator, are compelled to maintain cordial relations with the US for their own political survival. Unfortunately for Pakistan, the greatest face of terrorism on earth and enemy No.1 of the US Osama-bin-Laden was killed in a town in Pakistan through a swift and secret military operation by the US in October-2011. This exposed Pakistan's double-speak and tarnished its world image. It could neither defend itself nor vehemently criticise US action. This precarious position of Pakistan is a great diplomatic advantage for India, should India desire so and act accordingly. American and British secret agencies have amply proved Pakistan's secret support to terrorist activities. Another angle which adds to India's concern is Sino-Pak military exchanges and secret dealings on the border. It is a testing time for India to tackle both the countries diplomatically as well as generate world-wide support for her fight against terrorism.

At international level, the world will realise the importance of India some day and involve her in counter-terrorist activities. World community will also help us in our fight against terrorism. India has already initiated a process in this regard and has struck a deal with Israel, whose expert officers in counter-terrorism will train Indian Commandos. India has to curb terrorism with a firm hand. Government has introduced many special laws to deal with this problem. In the 1970s it was MISA that helped government to curb terrorism; in 1980s and 1990s, TADA was in force and today the government is armed with POTA.

But unfortunately there is no unanimity amongst the political leaders and intellectuals over the ways of tackling terrorism. The so-called secular and progressive people are opposing this law with an eye on the minority vote bank. These people also argue that punishment should be awarded to those whose terrorist actions are clearly established. It is also argued that government must first try to remove the real cause of terrorism, i.e.: poverty, unemployment, non-development, injustice and exploitation in the country. This is true, but is it possible in a country like India to achieve these goals to the fullest satisfaction of all and with speed? And is it possible to persuade the terrorists to take a break for sometime and wait till these goals are achieved? It is not a practical solution. Terrorism is clearly barbarism as it does not follow any rules. So stringent counter-terrorist measures have to be employed side by side with the speedier implementation of developmental schemes. For this, the so-called secular, humanist sections of the Indian intelligentsia, religious leaders and activists must come out of their colonial mindset and support POTA. Remember, counter-attacks and stringent actions are the only effective answers to the cult of gun. This was proved in Punjab and will be definitely help in Jammu and Kashmir. Besides, our law-enforcing agencies must also be geared up and enthused with national spirit to stand firm in any eventuality. Our own people who spy for the enemy, leak out secret information and give shelter to the terrorists in return of short-term and petty favours is very shameful. Equally shameful and disgraceful is escaping to the neighbouring countries of known culprits, criminals and terrorists from the jails or even before they are arrested. So, there is need to plug the loopholes in our legal and investigation systems.

In order to face the menace of terrorism, the internal security policy should be designed primarily as a deterrent policy and not merely as a defence policy. This has been done in the US and other western countries. This deterrence may be direct or indirect depending on the situation. Direct deterrence aims to deter an adversary by threatening to retaliate against the adversary for taking hostile action. This type of strategy is probably the most widely understood form of deterrence. It is also called "retaliation" or "punishment" strategies. It is true that this may not work against 'Suicide Bombers'; but is effective against terrorist leaders, financiers, supporters, radical clerics, and other members of terrorist groups who value their own life. For example, Tony Blair, former Prime Minister of Britain, announced his intention to pass legislation that would ban the "glorification of terrorism" after some clerics gave open speeches in Mosques against western policies about middle east. These clerics lived very lavish and comfortable life in London. Other laws were ineffective in this case. So, the "Glorification of Terrorism Law", passed in UK in March 2006, had an immediate effect. Rather than face prosecution at the hands of British authorities, prominent clerics left the United Kingdom for other countries, or changed their tune nearly overnight, renouncing previous calls to incite violence and speaking out against terrorism. It is high time that Indian government put the existing laws to their fullest use not allowing any loopholes. Another example is of Saudi government, which enhanced scrutiny of donors to some suspected organisations after 9/11 appears to have deterred some terrorist financing. The lesson for counter-terrorism is clear: The simple threat to punish individuals engaging in terrorist activity can have a significant deterrent effect on the support network. India should emulate the Saudi example.

Another strategy called indirect deterrence is one that deters by threatening to retaliate, not against terrorists themselves, but against something else that terrorists hold dear. While it is sometimes difficult to retaliate against specific terrorists, states may be able to threaten (or convince terrorists that their own actions might harm) other things they value such as their families, assets, and communities. An example of an indirect response strategy is Israel's past policy of demolishing the homes of suicide bombers' families. Israel could not threaten to punish suicide bombers themselves because they were dead after a successful attack, but it did retaliate against their families. This policy forced would-be suicide bombers to trade off the benefits of personal glory and martyrdom against the cost of homelessness for their immediate families. It has worked for Israel, but in India may raise human rights issue. But still it is worth giving a try.

Another strategy is to inflict demoralizing effect on the minds of the terrorists. Terrorists place great value on the operational success of their missions. Their aim is to kill a certain amount of soldiers/ men or damage a particular property in a given operation/mission. States can deter terrorism by convincing terrorists that operations are likely to fail. For this reason, simple internal security measures can deter terrorist attacks. Improving domestic intelligence and hardening key targets are strong deterrents to attack. Indeed, we know of many cases in which terrorists were deterred from carrying out an attack by the fear of failure. In short, states can deter terrorism by threatening failure at the tactical level. If terrorists fear that an attack will fail, they will be deterred from attempting it. This is not to undermine the importance of an alternative, strong and effective internal intelligence network.

Supportive action to the above strategy is that states can deter terrorism by steadfastly refusing to grant terrorist organisations their ultimate political demands. This is important in cases of abduction or hostages. If terrorist groups come to believe that a terror-based strategy will not help them to achieve their fundamental political goals, over time they may be deterred from choosing terrorism as a tactic. It may be for this reason that many States have adopted an official policy of refusing to negotiate with terrorists. The policy is not wholly driven by moral considerations, but rather by a strategic decision to deny terrorists the benefits of their actions. In addition, States also may be able to increase the credibility of their threats by developing a reputation for toughness. Terrorist groups should be less likely to target States that have a reputation for steadfastly refusing to negotiate with terrorists. In extreme cases, the government should not hesitate to take firm and direct action as done by Sri Lanka in case of LTTE.

In India's case the greatest obstacle in tackling terrorism in Jammu and Kashmir is the Article 370 in the Indian Constitution. It was a temporary provision inserted to tackle the fluid situation of 1947-48. But, once the constitution of Jammu and Kashmir and Indian Parliament have unequivocally declared that accession of Jammu and Kashmir is legal, final and irrevocable, this provision should have been removed. But political selfishness of the leaders of India and Jammu and Kashmir prevailed over nationalist interests and Article 370 continued. It is a myth and legal fallacy to call Article 370 a way of integration of Jammu and Kashmir into India and a symbol of our secular fabric. In fact this Article 370 has created more dissentions and encouraged separatist tendencies. It prevents Government of India from taking firm action on many issues. It discriminates between the people of Jammu and Kashmir and people of the rest of India. So, this provision must be removed from the constitution forthwith.

The last solution, which is different from the legal methods explained above, lies in the reform of religious faiths. This method is not the domain of any government, but solely the responsibility of common men, social and religious activists and reformists. The world today has been divided into 'Islamic and Non-Islamic', which is very unfortunate, but a harsh reality. Islam distinguishes between Muslims and non-Muslims. It does not recognise other faiths, other forms of worship, other cultures and civilisations. Islam should discard this ideology. It is high time that everybody realises that why would the God himself create so many religions if he wanted all men to follow one particular religion? So, all the religions are nothing but merely manifestations of the same Ultimate Truth. This truth must be filled in every mind, that will wipe out all hatred and ultimately all forms of terrorism. This is particularly true when Osama disappeared from the scene. It will be foolish to believe that terrorism has ended with the killing of Osama. In fact, the ideology may surface again, perhaps in more ugly form. So, it is important to wipe out that ideology through drastic religious reforms as explained above. Mahatma Gandhi refined his philosophy in and his philosophy of Satyagraha (Understanding the Ultimate Truth) and Ahimsa (Non-violence) and it has got world recognition today after the UN declared 2nd October as the "World Day of Non-violence". It is high time that the minds of the terrorists are indoctrinated with this philosophy so that the feelings of hatred, concept of superior-inferior and cult of weapon are wiped out from their minds. This will replace the feelings of Universal Brotherhood, Love and Respect for each other, which are more dignified, permanent and effective solution to the problem of Terrorism.

8

Naxalism and Violence

Kartik Lokhande

Historical Background of Naxalism

Before deliberating more upon the current situation of Naxalism, it will be appropriate to know certain historical aspects. The term Naxalism was coined after the 1967 Naxalbari armed uprising in the state of West Bengal. The uprising was led by Charu Mujumdar, Kanu Sanyal and others. Within Maoist ranks, however, only Charu Mujumdar is considered the leader of Naxalbari uprising against the big land owners. Kanu Sanyal is purposefully forgotten as he became a critic of Maoists in last years of his life. Considering the scale of uprising and greater threat perception, the then Government launched a police offensive called 'Operation Barga'. Under this operation, the police chased the armed villagers, who then fled to the forests and adopted guerrilla tactics.

Naxalbari uprising was followed by a similar violent uprising at Srikakulam. More armed uprisings were later reported from Birbhum, Mushahari, Kansksa or Sonapur. As the thought behind these uprisings had begun from Naxalbari, it came to be known as an ideology that was coined 'Naxalism' and the cadres were called Naxalites.

As Naxalism, in its original form, was a reaction by the oppressed and exploited masses to get justice with the help of arms, it received support from the intelligentsia in several parts of the country. Though it could not gain a wider popular support, it spread to other areas where there were people exploited by the big landlords. In some areas of Maharashtra and Madhya Pradesh, the tribals got their wages hiked for plucking Tendu leaves and cutting Bamboo, because of the pressure exerted by the Naxalites through their violent acts.

The police action that followed in these parts, clubbed with certain knee-jerk developmental responses from the Government side, slowly weaned the support base of the Naxalites. To add to this, there were differences of opinion amongst the Naxalite leaders which led to division in the rank and files. There was the period when cadres killed each other. This period was known as 'Black Chapter' amongst the ultra-lefts. During 1990s, the movement had become slow barring a few parts of the country including Maharashtra's bordering districts of Gadchiroli, Chandrapur, Bhandara, and Gondia.

In 1995, there were more than 40 groups of Naxalites active in various parts of the country with the prominent being Maoist Communist Centre of India (MCCI) in the Northern parts, People's War (PW) in Andhra Pradesh and some parts of Maharashtra, Madhya Pradesh and Odisha. By the end of the century, there was a situation, when Naxalism was considered as 'fading away romanticism.'

It was precisely towards the end of the century that the two major groups, MCCI and PW, started deliberating upon the possibility of merger to form one single group. During these periods, there was an agreement on advancing the Marxist-Leninist ideology to the Maoist thought. During the period of deliberations, the top leaders of MCCI and PW both met regularly at undisclosed locations and chalked out the course of action.

The agreement to the merger came towards 2002-03. It was during 2003-04 that the then Andhra Pradesh Government offered to hold talks with the Naxalites of PW. The Government also announced that there would not be any arrests of Naxalite cadres while the talks were in progress. Taking advantage of this golden opportunity, the Naxalite leaders congregated in Andhra Pradesh, rallied on roads, and also finalised the merger plan. On September 21, 2004, MCCI and PW merged to form the new Communist Party of India (Maoist). Obviously, the talks had failed in yielding desired positive results towards restoring peace from the Government as well as the ultra-Left side.

As one of the founding documents of CPI (Maoist) titled 'Hold High the Bright Red Banner of Marxism-Leninism-Maoism' states, "The clarion call of the great Naxalbari movement led by Comrade Charu Mujumdar proved to be a "Spring Thunder over India" as graphically described by CPC. It greatly unmasked the ugly face of the revisionist leadership of the CPI, CPI (M) brand. The powerful slogans like "China's Path is Our Path" and "Mao Tse Tung Thought is Our Thought" spread to the four corners of India and even other parts of the Sub-continent. Naxalbari thus marked a qualitative rupture with age-old revisionism in the Indian communist movement and firmly established the universal truth of MLM Thought in India. From then on, MLM Thought had become a demarcating line between revisionists and genuine revolutionaries in India. Thus "Naxalbari path, the only path" became an ever-resounding slogan. This movement further inspired and attracted a completely new generation of revolutionary communist forces from among the masses of workers, peasants, students, youth, women and intellectuals towards the ideology of MLM Thought."

Within seven years of its formation, CPI (Maoist) has spread its network as well as its ideology in 16 states and most of which were from the Eastern side of India. In fact, today 'the revolutionary movement' has assumed enormity with its spread to large tracts of backward countryside. It has a well-knit party structure, Army and vast mass base.

Still, there are groups who call themselves Naxalites but did not join the Maoists ideology. Besides, there are other splinter groups that are the results of differences within ultra-Left ideology groups. One such example is Tritiya Prastuti Committee active in Jharkhand. It was formed as a number of cadres of CPI (Maoist) in Jharkhand walked out complaining domination of Yadav caste in decision-making process. The cadres of Tritiya Prastuti Committee mostly belong to Dalit, Bhokta, Turi, Badai, Oraon, and Ghanju communities. It is also posing a threat to Maoists since its inception, Tritiya Prastuti Committee has indulged in fratricidal clashes with CPI (Maoist) and other Maoist outfits including Jharkhand Liberation Tigers.

Despite these fratricidal clashes, CPI (Maoist) has emerged as one of the most active Maoist parties in South Asia. The graph of violent activities that range from killing policemen and alleged police informers to destroying roads, communication towers, to jailbreaks to arms loots, has been rising. At present, as per the Government estimates, the Maoists have presence in almost 40 per cent geographical area of the country. By sheer expanse, it has become the priority task for the security agencies. As far as its estimated manpower is concerned, the CPI (Maoist) has anywhere between 18,000 and 21,000 armed cadres across the country with most of them being active in states of Chhattisgarh and Jharkhand that are again mineral rich.

Probably, for this reason, in 2008, Prime Minister Dr Manmohan Singh said, "The Naxal groups are targeting all aspects of economic activity, including vital infrastructure so as to cripple transport and logistical capabilities and slow down any development. We cannot rest in peace until we have eliminated this virus".

Apart from working in the tribal-dominated areas that also have good mineral and forest reserves, the Maoists have been consistently working on the plan to encircle the cities from the countryside. In an attempt to create its network in the urban centres, the Maoists have formed several front organisations and have been targeting the unemployed youths and labour class. In semi-urban centres, CPI (Maoist) has been spreading its ideology amongst the peasants and labour class.

Organisationally, CPI (Maoist) has a well-defined structure. Maoists have State Committees in Punjab, Maharashtra, Delhi, Uttar Pradesh, Haryana, Jharkhand, Bihar, Chhattisgarh, Odisha, Tamil Nadu, Karnataka, and Andhra Pradesh. These states are governed by the Regional Bureaus. North Regional Bureau, for instance, looks after Delhi, Punjab, Haryana, Bihar, and Uttar Pradesh. South-Western Regional Bureau has network in

Maharashtra, Karnataka, Tamil Nadu, and Kerala under its command. Eastern Regional Bureau comprises Assam, West Bengal, Jharkhand and coastal belt. Central Regional Bureau has command over Andhra Pradesh and three special zonal committees. There is also an independent Regional Bureau for Odisha and Chhattisgarh.

There are three special zonal committees for North Telangana, Dandakaranya, and Andhra Pradesh-Odisha Border. For Uttar Bihar, Uttar Pradesh, and Uttaranchal, there is a 3-U Special Area Committee. Apart from these, there is a Central Military Commission in the CPI (Maoist) that monitors all the military violent actions of the cadres. Before merger, there was a restricted number of cadres in a dalam (group). However, now, the Maoists are in the process of developing their own army and if the documents seized so far by the security agencies provide any indication, the Maoists have training and arms units also.

Thus, from Naxalism to Maoism, the Left Wing Extremists in India have not only advanced themselves ideologically but also have reoriented their strategy and tactics.

Though the Maoists have stated in their founding documents that they had advanced to the Maoist thought, the Communists in India think of Maoists as a bunch of anarchists who are out to achieve massive social revolution with the use of gun. In fact, a CPI-ML leader had recently stated that CPI-ML had got carried away by the adventurist attitude by taking to arms as the only means of bringing out social revolution. However, Maoists are working on the plans laid out in the founding documents.

Considering the faster ideological advance and plans drawn up to work on the urban perspective, it would not be premature to say that in the years to come, the Maoists would advance themselves to the thoughts of Che Guevara, and General Vo Nguyen Giap.

MLM Philosophy

Marxism-Leninism-Maoism or MLM advancement is one of the core philosophies of CPI (Maoist). The advancement is well explained in their document 'Hold High the Bright Red Banner of Marxism-Leninism-Maoism' by the CPI (Maoist) Central Committee. Here is a brief look at it.

Maoists have analysed the contribution of Marx, Lenin, and Mao towards the cause of establishing the dictatorship of the proletariat. As the above-mentioned Maoist document states, "Marx developed the theory of the dictatorship of the proletariat as a form of rule of the proletariat and as a method of overthrowing the rule of capital by force. . . . In other words, the proletariat should use revolutionary means to seize state power, smash the military bureaucratic machine of the bourgeoisie and establish the dictatorship of the proletariat to replace the dictatorship of the bourgeoisie."

As the Maoist organisations and even the Communist organisations believe across the world, Lenin advanced the Marxist thought by analyzing it as well as by adding 'value' to it. Lenin provided not only the concept and practice of party building, but also the alliances with other similar forces and building a mesh of organisations through which the party functioned 'clandestinely'.

As the CPI (Maoist) points out, "Lenin made a path-breaking leap in the concept and practice of Party building, which is a great addition to the arsenal of Marxism. Lenin considered it of prime importance for the proletariat to establish its own genuinely revolutionary political party, which completely breaks with opportunism, that is, a Communist Party, if the proletarian revolution is to be carried through, and the dictatorship of the proletariat established and consolidated. He brilliantly summed up the need for the party in the famous phrase "*The Proletariat, in its struggle for power, has no weapon other than organisation*".

The next stage to which the Marxist-Leninist thought advanced is Maoism. As is known to all and written 'n' number of times by innumerable writers, Mao Tse Tung believed in furthering the cause of proletariat's struggle for power to the stage of centralism, which is often mentioned by the critiques as the domination of an individual over the party that assumes power.

The CPI (Maoist) quotes Mao on centralism in its document, "Without democracy there can't be correct centralism because centralism can't be established when people have divergent views and don't have unity of understanding. What is meant by centralism? First, there must be concentration of correct ideas. Unity of understanding, of policy, plan, command and action is attained on the basis of concentrating correct ideas. This is unity through centralism. But if all those concerned are still not clear about the problems, if their opinions are still unexpressed or their anger is still not vented, how can you achieve this unity through centralism? Without democracy, it is impossible to sum up experience correctly. Without democracy, without ideas coming from the masses, it is impossible to formulate good lines, principles, policies or methods."

Apart from explaining the relation between centralism and democracy, Mao has also prescribed three 'Magic Weapons' namely the Party, the Army, and the United Front.

After taking a brief look at the Marxism-Leninism-Maoism (MLM) philosophy of the CPI (Maoist), one gets an idea of the goal towards which the Maoists in India are working. As has been reiterated by the Maoists in their different documents, they have been consistently following Mao's prescription of three 'Magic Weapons'. One can find a reflection of this in their party structure as well as the conscious building of party structure. As has been mentioned earlier in the paper, the Maoists are close to making their own Army. At present, they have attained the level of training their cadres on the lines of military squads, and equipping them with strategic as well as tactical training. The recent ambushes in which the Maoists killed several policemen across the country are an indication of this.

In fact, in one of its documents, the Union Home Ministry has pointed out that the CPI (Maoist) party structure at the central level consists of Politbureau (PB), Central Committee (CC), and Central Military Commission (CMC). The CMC has different units under its command which include Central Technical Committee, Regional Commands, Special Action Teams, Military Intelligence, Publications and Editorial Board of 'Jung' (the military magazine), Central Military Instructors Team, Communications, Tactical Counter Offensive Campaign, Peoples Liberation Guerilla Army (PLGA).

CPI (Maoist) Founding Documents and 9th Unity Congress Resolutions

After understanding advancement of Left Wing Extremists to Maoist line, one gets a better insight into their line of action and plans from the CPI (Maoist) founding documents as well as from the resolutions passed in the 9th Unity Congress held in February 2007 somewhere deep in forests of Jharkhand.

CPI (Maoist) has five founding documents: Hold High the Bright Red Banner of Marxism-Leninism-Maoism or the MLM pamphlet, Political Resolution, Party Programme, and Strategy and Tactics of the Indian Revolution, and the Party Constitution. Besides, they have an important document titled 'Urban Perspective' explaining the strategy of penetrating into urban areas towards achieving the final objective set by Mao to 'capture' the cities. Following the line of thought, CPI (Maoist) held the 9th Unity Congress in which it passed various resolutions that explain the plan and philosophy of Maoists towards several aspects.

Among the founding documents, as explained above, MLM pamphlet explains philosophically the background of advancing to Maoist line and future course of action based on it. Political Resolution combines experiences of the erstwhile PW and MCCI. While examining the international situation, this resolution calls Asia, Africa, and Latin America as the storm-centres of revolution apart from voicing support to 'people's war' in Nepal, Peru, Philippines and Turkey. It also examines the situation within India. The Party Constitution mainly concentrates on organisational matters of CPI (Maoist) and guiding principles. The Constitution of CPI (Maoist) is based on 'Bolshevik principles of democratic centralism, with the core comprising of professional revolutionaries.' The document calls for having a wide network of part timers to facilitate the Party existence deep within the masses.

The document titled 'Party Programme' focuses on analyzing the situation within India as well as outlining the CPI (Maoist) programme if it captures power. One can make a fair guess about it from the developments in Nepal where the Maoists gained power for a short while. CPI (Maoist) programme is more of a political party's manifesto promising several things. Some of them include abolishing the existing educational system, doing away with current tax system, confiscating all banks, business enterprises and companies 'of imperialist capital and abrogate all imperialist debt', nullifying 'unequal treaties and agreements with imperialist countries', confiscating capital of all enterprises apart from movable and immovable properties of 'comprador bureaucratic bourgeoisie', taking over authority and administration of all monopoly industries and trades, confiscating all land belonging to landlords and religious institutions and its redistribution among landless poor peasants and agricultural labourers, ensuring remunerative prices for agricultural products etc.

Whereas, the 'Strategy and Tactics of Indian Revolution' analyses Indian society's class character, and outlines the strategy of capturing political power by armed force. Strategy part also focuses on building agrarian revolution, constituting a People's Army/Militia, securing 'liberated' areas, etc. The tactics part concentrates on building the party, United Front, tactics with regard to various 'nationalities', work in urban areas, intensifying the protracted people's war. Considering the standard confines for a paper, it would not be appropriate to delve into greater details on various Maoist documents, but broader mention of the contents would suffice the need.

As far as 9th Unity Congress is concerned, several resolutions were passed. These included resolutions on farmers' suicides, nationality struggles, State violence against women, and resolutions against death penalty, Hindu fascism, special economic zones and displacement, and Dalit killings at Khairlanji in Maharashtra. As is explained from the topics of the resolutions, they focused on related issues and appealed various targeted sections to participate in and 'intensify the armed struggle to overthrow semi-colonial, semi-feudal system'. During the 9th Unity Congress, the Cadres were also asked to convert prisons into political universities and build party organisation in jails, of which a reflection was seen in Jehanabad jailbreak incident and incidents of prisoners taking control of prisons at Beur and Dantewada for a while.

The Government Philosophy and Programmes

To develop a complete picture of the situation today, one needs to understand the State philosophy apart from the Maoist philosophy.

A democratic republic, India has got a unique persona with its multi-lingual, multi-religious, multi-cultural fabric. During the pre-Independence period, there was almost a classless freedom struggle against the Britishers, who were outsiders ruling India. The post-

Independence period saw a sea change. In fact, the British rulers played their game coyly and got India partitioned to pave way for a Muslim country, which gave birth to not only a hostile neighbour but also led to disturbing the harmonious co-existence within India.

Post-Independence era saw India grow impressively. Though the political system and delayed reforms on various vital counts, clubbed with corrupt practices, eventually led to a 'not-so-pleasant' situation; it did not alter India's foundation of a welfare state. With the foundation, there came several responsibilities of ensuring welfare of various societal components. The Government, or the Indian State, has been doing so while facing the hurdles created by an era of neglect towards certain evils like corruption and bureaucrat-politician nexus. The exceptions to this general picture are the ones who are still fighting within the system to bring about the desired positive change. More recently, with the anti-corruption movement led by noted Gandhian Anna Hazare, the issue of corruption again occupied centre-stage of public discourse, thereby mounting pressure on the Government to effect certain vital policy changes.

As far as dealing with the Maoists-or for that matter any insurgent group-is concerned, any nation-state has to have a clear view and that view obviously tends to act against the perceived threat to the largesse in any form. From time to time, the Indian Government has tried to find out solutions to the erstwhile Naxalite and now the Maoist menace. However, most of the times, it could not sustain tempo of implementing various welfare measures considering the Left Wing Extremism as more of a socio-economic problem than a security challenge. Off late, based upon the heightened threat perception from the Maoists, the Government has started treating it as the biggest internal security threat, and has chalked out a multi-pronged strategy to deal with it.

As the document of Naxal Management Division under the Ministry of Home Affairs, points out, the Government has a clearly defined policy to combat the challenge posed by the Naxalite/ Maoist menace. This particular policy acts as guideline in acting against the banned outfit of CPI (Maoist). As per the policy, the Government warns to deal sternly with the Maoists indulging in violence. Also, it has clear-cut guideline that unless the Maoists abjure violence, there will not be any talks.

If one considers that nation is an identity formed by the diverse mass of population, then the Government, irrespective of any party leading it, has to act so as to protect the interests and security of the larger people who are not on the side of the rebel or insurgent groups. However, at the same time, it cannot go on killing all insurgents if they are home-grown. The insurgency within the nation is traditionally a result of discontent or discord against the nation-state over one or the other issue. Hence, while dealing with internal security threat like the Maoists, the Government has resorted to various other options too including initiating socio-economic measures, leaving the option of talks open if the insurgents abjure violence, and also exploring employment opportunities.

Other policies of the Indian Government, as explained in the Naxal Management Division document, include addressing Maoist 'menace' simultaneously on political, security, development and public perception management fronts in a holistic manner; asking the states to adopt a collective approach and pursue a coordinated response to counter Maoists; calling the states to improve police response and pursue effective and sustained police action against the Maoists and their infrastructure individually and jointly etc. As the country has a democratic set up, the role of political parties is also important. Accordingly, the Government has asked the political parties to strengthen their cadre base in Maoist-affected areas so that potential youth support to the banned group in such pockets could be weaned away from the path of Maoist ideology.

While there is no system of accountability of the masses or the insurgent groups to the people across the world, the democratic Government is answerable to all. Considering this point, the Indian Government has asked its states where Maoists have not committed any violent act, to have a different approach with special focus on accelerated socio-economic development of the backward areas and regular interaction with NGOs, intelligentsia, civil society groups. The State Governments are also asked to accord higher priority in their annual plans to ensure faster socio-economic development of affected areas, with emphasis on distributing land to landless poor as part of speedy implementation of land reforms, development of physical infrastructure like roads, communication, power, and making available employment opportunities to youth there.

In a democratic set up, the Government assumes the responsibility as a custodian of the interest of citizens. If the insurgents come from among the citizens, the Government cannot act against them directly without offering them any opportunity. As a part of this, the Government has also offered surrender and rehabilitation policy for Naxalites/Maoists. In reaction to Left Wing Extremists' violence, the Government included CPI (Maoist) and all its formations in the list of banned terrorist organisations under Unlawful Activities (Prevention) Act, 1967.

As part of its counter-propaganda to Maoists, the Government has started inserting advertisements in various newspapers across the country and also on different television channels highlighting killings of innocent people, destruction of school buildings, and economic infrastructure including damage caused to railways. Between 2005 and 2011, as per the Government's estimates, the Maoists destroyed 272 schools, and killed 3,770 civilians. The Government has also highlighted exploitation of women cadres and children by the Maoists.

Summing up, the Government is acting on a philosophy of welfare state, but it is needs to be more alert about the excesses of the system and pilferage of funds meant to carry out welfare and developmental activities.

Chhattisgarh and Lalgarh : Salwa Judum and People's Militia

Putting Salwa Judum and the Maoists' People's Militia together may not be palatable for several sections. However, when it comes to violence, especially after understanding the philosophy, it becomes a necessity to examine violence inflicted by both the sides.

As is widely known, Salwa Judum was started as an armed mass resistance against the Maoists in Chhattisgarh. Sponsored by Chhattisgarh Government, Mahendra Karma of Congress had taken a lead in preparing the mass resistance group. Many believe that first the tribals had resisted Maoists who used to terrorise them at gun point. Later, the BJP-led Government adopted it as a strategy and tactic to counter Maoists. The move was actually an internationally recognised War Zone Policy. When the State has to have control over areas where the insurgents draw their strength mostly from local populace, the State also tries to involve the locals.

However, within a couple of years of growth of Salwa Judum (which literally means peace movement) to several tribals armed against the Maoists, the Government attracted criticism mainly because members of the group resorted to brutality against fellow tribals. It was a matter of debate as to how many of those killed by Salwa Judum activists were actually Maoist cadres. Civil society groups took up the cause of opposing Salwa Judum and even the matter went for hearing to the National Human Rights Commission as well as the courts of law. More recently, the Supreme Court disapproved the idea of having State-backed counter-resistance groups of tribals.

Owing to resistance to the Maoists, Salwa Judum activists also faced a backlash and the Government put them in refugee camps. To ensure safety and security of the activists in camps, more tribals were armed. Salwa Judum activists were later given the status of Special Police Officers. The Maoists, too, intensified their actions against Salwa Judum activists and killed several of them. South Asia Terrorism Portal data shows that between June 2005 and July 2009, Maoists killed 246 Salwa Judum activists.

While Chhattisgarh was known more for Salwa Judum, Lalgarh in West Bengal also hits the headlines for the Maoists' initiative of building People's Militia. Actually, People's Militia was not a new concept for Left Wing Extremists. It was a concept that was implemented several times in different areas on a varying scale, even by the Naxalites. However, what Lalgarh brought to fore was the fact that since inception, the CPI (Maoist) had been aggressively implementing the policy of building People's Militia. South Asia Terrorism Portal data reveals that between February 2004 and July 2009, total 135 incidents had taken place involving People's Militia through which the Maoists affected loot of arms from police stations, killing people, former cadres, and policemen.

To build the People's Militia, Maoists stuck to their textbooks that prescribe the stages of protracted people's war-survey, struggle, resistance, guerrilla action, holding the area and expanding it. Maoists follow Mao, Che Guevara, and General Vo Nguyen Giap's strategies and tactics. Accordingly, their attempts to involve the people comprise three stages:

1. Work to earn popular support through ideological indoctrination and attacks on Government establishments.
2. Escalating attacks against the Government and targeting security forces and vital establishments.
3. Adopting conventional warfare and deploying its forces to capture cities and overthrow the Government to seize complete control of a country.

In an interview to a magazine, CPI (Maoist) General Secretary Ganapathy was asked a question: 'Is your violence for self-defence or to grab state power?' Ganapathy had replied, "Strictly speaking, you cannot separate the two. In the long-term perspective, or ultimately, our goal is to seize state power without which it is impossible to liberate the people of our country from the clutches of imperialism, feudalism, and the big comprador bourgeoisie, that is, change the existing unjust socio-economic system."

Given the violence and perceived threat of its escalation in the near future, with neither the Maoists nor the Government being in a mood to take up the cause of serving the real interests of the people, it becomes primary responsibility of civil society groups and conscientious individuals to come up with a solution so as to first halt the violence from both the sides and then resolve the issues concerning the people in newly created disturbed areas.

Operation Green Hunt, the Government Offensive

After recognizing the Maoists as the biggest internal security threat, the Central Government announced that it would launch an anti-Maoist offensive towards the end of the year 2009. After postponing its launch at least thrice, the Government started it silently.

Prior to launching the operation, which is believed to have been code-named Operation Green Hunt, the Ministry of Home Affairs released a study regarding the affected areas. As per the study, out of total 231 districts affected by Maoist violence, 70 were badly affected. Among 70 districts, 40 were worst affected. Based on this study, the Government decided to launch operation in 11 areas in 40 districts. Already, 40 battalions were deployed in these areas, and under the operation, the Government planned to deploy

30 more. As has already been said by the Government officials while talking to different media banners, the operation would be a reply to the protracted people's war of the Maoists, and hence it would be a long battle that may last for a period anywhere between three and five years.

If one goes by media reports, one finds that Green Hunt is a part of wider operation code-named Godavari or Siddharth. Operation Green Hunt currently comprises seven phases. In the first two phases, the security personnel would try to encircle Abujhmarh, which is considered a citadel of the Maoists. Abujhmarh, which literally means 'unknown land', would be the concentration of forces that move from two directions, Chhattisgarh and Maharashtra. From Chhattisgarh, forces have already started moving ahead from Bijapur towards Dantewada, Narainpur, and Bastar, and then Abujhmarh. From Maharashtra end, forces are likely to move from Gadchiroli towards Abujhmarh.

Though there are talks of Indian Army and Indian Air Force to be involved at a later stage, the Government has not supported it, for the fear of spreading its forces thin. The Government has cleared involvement of Indian Air Force helicopters in anti-Maoist operations only for dropping the troops, media reports say. At present, various security analysis groups in the country have warned the Government against calling for the Army's involvement in anti-Maoist operations. Still, reports are appearing in the newspapers that the Indian Army has sought around 2,000 acres of land near Bilaspur to set up a brigade headquarters. Also, there are talks of carpet security plan of Chhattisgarh Government. The Centre has asked affected States to take an initiative and has assured them support.

As far as the Government's own admission of its policy for combating the Maoists is concerned, it states," The Government of India believes in a holistic long-term policy in the areas of security, development, ensuring rights of local communities, improving governance and perception management to combat LWE. Most of the security related measures, apart from deployment of CAPFs, are aimed at assisting capacity building by the State forces. On the development front, an Integrated Action Plan covering 78 affected districts aimed at providing public infrastructure and services is under implementation. Further, an ambitious Road Development

Plan has been envisaged for LWE areas. An Empowered Group of Officers closely monitors the progress of flagship schemes. Special emphasis is being laid on implementation of Forest Rights Act and ensuring entitlement of local communities over Minor Forest Produce."

However, while the Government has been preparing for the offensive against them, the Maoists were also working consistently to gain an insight of related developments. If one goes through news reports and the Maoist documents seized by the police machinery across the country, it is revealed that the Maoists knew about the offensive way back in August 2006. The Maoists' mouthpiece People's March magazine had an article in its August-September 2006 issue under the title 'Government prepares for a massive clamp down on Maoists'.

Further, in its June 12, 2009, Politbureau Circular titled 'Post-election Situation: Our Tasks', CPI (Maoist) assessed 'threat from the Government', and clearly mentions about blueprint of the Centre about offensive. It stated that all-round preparations are in final stage for launching massive brutal offensive on guerrilla zones and guerrilla bases. It advised Maoist cadres to aggravate the situation and create more difficulties for Centre's forces by expanding guerrilla war to newer areas and intensify mass resistance in existing areas to disperse forces over sufficiently wider areas to divert forces from attacking guerrilla bases and organs of political power. It recognised that Centre had severe difficulties in implementing offensive. It revealed Maoist plans to escalate violence across areas of dominance as well as extending such activities to newer areas.

Besides, the Maoists were augmenting their fire power as well as manpower sensing the nature of the Government offensive. A register of the Naxals, dated February 13, 2007, seized recently by Central security agencies, revealed that Maoists had spent Rs 11,05,000 on buying 13 pieces of 0.315 rifle and Rs 13.65 lakh on seven pieces of 30.06 rifles. Further, the security agencies last year recovered 92 AK-47, 18 AK-56, Pakistan-made Pica guns and Israeli sniper guns from Maoist camps.

While the Maoists in West Bengal, Uttar Pradesh, and Madhya Pradesh are reportedly using locally manufactured arms, the Maoist groups in Bihar, Jharkhand, and Andhra Pradesh use foreign small arms including those from China. This indicates the Maoists' attempts to expand their support base and form alliances that go beyond the borders of India. As the FICCI report on security and terrorism states, "It may be taken into account that the Maoists have developed connectivity with arms suppliers in Thailand, Cambodia, and Vietnam. The Maoists command control of certain coastal areas in West Bengal, Odisha, and Andhra Pradesh through which weapons are smuggled in." It clearly shows the level of preparations of the Maoists to counter the Indian Government's offensive against them.

Sensing that the Maoists might be arming the tribals for what they call a protracted people's war, the Government has off late started saying that it would expedite development in affected areas to erode the Maoists' support base. The development initiatives would be launched through restoration of administration, once the forces cleared the areas of Maoists. The Government move is aimed at redressing the grievances of the people of affected areas. How far the Government's 'clear and hold' policy succeeds and how the Maoists react to it, remains to be seen.

For the sake of records, the Government has denied existence of Operation Green Hunt. According to a February 2012 document of Ministry of Home Affairs, "The word 'Operation Green Hunt' does not exist in any record of the Ministry of Home Affairs. In fact, there is no such operation at all, for the simple reason that the Ministry of Home Affairs does not plan or execute operations. Law and Order being state subjects, all Anti-naxal operations are planned by the State forces, assisted by the Central forces. The term 'Operation Green Hunt', it seems, was used for a local operation in Bastar Range in Chhattisgarh. The operation was aimed at busting naxal dens in Bastar forests existing in green camouflage tents. But the Maoist propagandists and Front Organisations, in a masterly strategy, attributed it ad nauseam, to the Central Government, conjuring up visions of hapless adivasis being targeted by the Government machinery. It needs to be recognised that this propaganda was played out very skillfully, so much so that, many in the mainstream media also believe there is a 'Operation Green Hunt'. The fact, however, remains that all operations are planned/ led by State forces and inter-state operations are planned by the

States concerned, in consultation with the Central Armed Police Forces. Further, it is also a fact that far more civilians/SF's are killed by naxalites than naxalites by SF's, contrary to the propaganda that security forces commit atrocities on innocents."

In the recent past, that is, in 2010 and 2011, the Government has been successful in gunning down top Maoist leaders like Azad and Kishenji apart from putting behind bars several others including four Polit Bureau members Kobad Ghandy, Narayan Sanyal, Amit Bagchi, and Sushil Rai. This has led to a relative calm from Maoists' side. The situation in Maoist camp is best described in a CPI (Maoist) statement, which pointed out that in 2011 alone, the party lost 150 members and more than 20 of its leaders were arrested.

In an interview given to 'The Week' magazine in December 2011, Maoist sympathiser Varavara Rao reacted to this and said, "These (Azad and Kishenji) are big losses, which are not easy to replace. But, they brought hundreds of others into the party. By now, there are many leaders who have come up," indicating that the party had not given up and the calm in Maoist camp might be momentary.

The Complex Society Reacts to Anti-Maoist Offensive

The anti-Maoist offensive of the Government has attracted criticism from civil society groups for the fear of escalation of violence in which tribals would be the main casualty. Certain critical sections have dubbed the offensive as 'Operation Blind Hunt' while some have even objected to the use of word 'Hunt'. Whereas, among the common people, the Government has been successful in engraving the significance of the operation as is evident from the public comments published in several newspapers. It would be appropriate to discuss them one by one.

As is known to many now, the intellectuals, or most of them, are opposed to the anti-Maoist offensive. These intellectuals range from Booker prize winner author Arundhati Roy to other literary figures from Kolkata to the professors of Social Sciences and Sociology at Jawaharlal Nehru University and Delhi University. The organisations that are opposed to the offensive also range from mainstream Communist parties to comparatively smaller civil society groups like Sanhati. The Internet is flooded with online petitions against the anti-Maoist offensive. These petitions are signed by well-known figures including Arundhati Roy, Noam Chomsky, and others.

These intellectuals, in their petitions or articles, have condemned the violence perpetrated by the Maoists but have also opposed the anti-Maoist offensive citing the reason that it would not be in the interest of the nation. Most of them have asked the Government to re-think the move given the fact that Maoists operate in the vacuum created by inefficiency and inadequacy of the administration as well as political class. Against this backdrop, the civil society groups have also asked the Government to first expedite the developmental works in the affected areas. Some groups have even suggested the Government to take a lead and initiate peace talks with the Maoists.

The intellectuals have opposed the anti-Maoist offensive and have tagged it with an appeal for the Government to halt it. But, they have failed in providing alternative course of action or an all-inclusive solution that would benefit larger part of the society. As a result, the intellectuals have ended up indirectly supporting Maoist cause, and have placed themselves on the radar of Intelligence agencies. Besides, while attacking only the Government in their expression of thought, the intellectuals have recognised the Government as the custodian of interests of countrymen. At the same time, intellectuals have rejected the notion that Maoists stand for the people.

While, the civil society groups and celebrated intellectuals are opposed to the offensive, the Maoists too are trying to create a negative impression about the Government among the masses. Sample this: In one of the latest press releases by the CPI (Maoist) displayed on a few pro-Maoist websites, Maoist top rank has accused P Chidambaram, Union Home Minister, for his alleged past links with the mining group Vedanta, which is setting up a mine in Maoist-affected area. Besides, the Maoists have been hammering for quite some time that the Government offensive against them was nothing but a ploy to clear the resistance of the people to 'plunder of resources in tribal-dominated areas' by the multi-national corporations and mining giants.

In reply to an Economic and Political Weekly article, an unnamed CPI (Maoist) spokesperson had stated at one place that 'the plan of rulers is to evict adivasis from the region and settle them elsewhere permanently.... We oppose only such development projects that harm the interests of adivasis, facilitiate the unhindered exploitation of the region's wealth, displace the indigenous tribes and the inhabitants of the forests from their homes and lands, and destroy their way of living and their culture. It is a misgiving that we are opposed to every kind of road construction or that we disrupt power supply and communication'. Though it was more of an attempt to explain the Maoists' stand on development, the Maoist spokesperson could not resist from targeting the Government.

As a reaction to the launch of Operation Green Hunt, the Maoists have stepped up their activities especially in Chhattisgarh, Jharkhand, and Odisha. In the past couple of weeks, there were reports of Maoist violence from newer areas also. In a bid to damage the morale of the security personnel advancing towards Abujhmarh, the Maoists have been attacking the policemen in different parts of the country.

This has had its impact on the policemen in certain pockets, as could be assessed from media reports that the cops are hesitant to go on long range patrolling in Maoist-affected areas. In fact, if one goes at the highest levels, the celebrated supercop K.P.S. Gill has also asked the Government if it wanted the country's troops to get stuck in Maoist-affected areas just like the American troops got stuck in Afghanistan?

Several security experts also have advised the Government to tread cautiously. In his article 'Floundering in a Long War', Ajit Kumar Singh, Research Associate, Institute for Conflict Management, has noted that "Hurried and ill-planned operations, using troops that are unfamiliar with local conditions, lacking hard intelligence, in many cases, under-trained, ill-prepared and under-equipped, and in all cases, lacking the critical mass of manpower needed to saturate the areas in which the Maoists have established their disruptive dominance. The challenge of Maoist extremism is not insurmountable. But hasty and misdirected initiatives, far from advancing resolution, will undermine the legitimacy and authority of the Forces and infinitely compound the basic problems themselves."

Before the launch of anti-Maoist offensive the Government had been saying about restoring development in the backward regions. However, that also had been attacked by the intellectuals. Nandini Chandra, Guest Contributor, Sanhati, in her paper presented at Left Forum-2009, had stated, "We are again and again being asked to see the Maoists as a furtive force lurking 'behind the curtain' coming to the people's rescue, but also establishing simultaneously that the people and the Maoists cannot be one and the same. The welfarist view, however noble, does not seem very realistic since it says nothing about tackling the forces of speculative private capital which are ruling the State currently." As if taking a cue from this observation, Left parties questioned the propriety of 'waging a war against own countrymen' when the Government had failed in resolving the problems haunting the people especially in the post-liberalisation era. However, the Left parties' approach appeared to be dual as they had advocated a crackdown on the Maoists in Lalgarh in West Bengal. This crackdown, or Operation Lalgarh, was apparently a result of threat posed to political existence of Communist Party and to cover up its failure in addressing popular grievances as was evident from participation of people in Maoist-led activities.

The Right wingers, who have always been critical of the Maoists, have welcomed the Government offensive. According to them, Maoists deserve no mercy as they have killed several tribals and innocent civilians in the name of being police informers. Hence, if there is a Government offensive, it needs to be implemented with full force. In one of his statements, Vishwa Hindu Parishad's then International President Ashok Singhal had urged the Central Government to even make use of Army and the Air Force 'to finish off Maoists who are wreaking havoc in the country with open support from China.' The articles penned by Rightist thinkers appearing in media make a clear suggestion that the Maoists should be crushed and their urban network must be busted by plugging the support mechanisms. While doing so, some Rightist thinkers have suggested adopting a softer developmental approach for the people in affected areas.

The industrial groups are slightly cautious about commenting on the anti-Maoist offensive. As the FICCI report on security and terrorism makes a point, "A purely security related approach to dealing with Naxalism is unlikely to succeed. States like Andhra Pradesh and Bihar have still not implemented land reforms. Several political groups maintain understanding with the Naxalites. And sections of urban intelligentsia are sympathetic to the Naxalite cause....There is hardly any aerial surveillance, electronic monitoring mechanism to intercept communication network of Maoists." Thus, the report has welcomed the offensive and has made suggestions to add value to it from security point of view as well as from development point of view.

The common man, whose identity differs from individual to individual and from organisation to organisation, also has something to say on the anti-Maoist offensive as is evident from the letters published in various newspapers. In major urban centres, the common man has adopted a cautious approach while making a comment on the issue. There, the letters published in newspapers show that the urban populace feels strongly for the tribals in 'War Zone' from human rights point of view. Some have even suggested halting the operation. Whereas, the comment of readers in newspapers in other urban centres as well as in vernacular press, are generally supportive of the Government move. In fact, certain letters have expressed the sentiment that the Government should initiate the action like the one by Sri Lankan Government against the Liberation Tigers of Tamil Eelam.

However, one must say, almost all the reactions fail in making vital suggestions that would lead to development in the Maoist-affected areas and restoration of peace in place of violence. In absence of attempts at making suggestions that would eventually lead to stopping the violence from both the sides, any other reaction from any constituent of the society would actually mean supporting one side or the other. And, thus, it would lead the situation nowhere near the cause of stopping the violence.

Conclusion and Some Suggestions

While examining various aspects associated with Maoism and related violence in the country, one thing becomes clear that there is certainly an atmosphere of distrust among the general public about the Government's existing model of governance as well as about the model proposed by the Maoists. The distrust about the Government's current model of governance has developed due to geographical as well as sectoral pockets that have suffered decades-long neglect. And, the distrust about the model proposed by the Maoists is mainly due to the path of violence they have chosen to overthrow the existing system. Any model that is based either on oppression or on violence is bound to yield discontent in longer run.

One also concludes that the Maoists operate in vacuum created by near-lack of developmental attitude and necessary administrative as well as security support. This is generally accepted by various quarters. Planning Commission of India's Expert Group report on Development Challenges in Extremist Affected Areas-2008, which discusses internal security situation vis-à-vis Maoist spread, observes that 'excepting knee-jerk responses, there had not been any sustained administrative and developmental action, including to eliminate the causes and reduce the discontent of masses'.

The introduction part of Naxal Management Division, Ministry of Home Affairs, Government of India, reads, "In areas under Maoist domination, absence of governance becomes a self-fulfilling prophecy since the delivery systems are extinguished through killings and intimidation. This is the first step in the strategy of the Maoists to seek to control the countryside. In the meanwhile, many Front Organisations are created to facilitate mass-mobilisation in semi-urban and urban areas through ostensibly democratic means. Most of the Front Organisations are led by well-educated intellectuals with a firm belief in Maoist insurgency doctrine. These ideologues function as masks to cover the violent nature of CPI (Maoist) ideology. They form propaganda/disinformation machinery of the party."

"By exploiting the societal grievances of India's tribal people, the multitudinous poor, women, and the lower castes, which in many cases are genuine, the Maoists have worked up anger and antagonism against the State to their advantage. Many of the cadres do not subscribe to any ideology but are into the movement to take advantage of the power that a gun can draw in a lawless land," states the FICCI report on security and terrorism.

Even the Maoists do not hesitate from pointing out their aims of taking advantage of multi-level contradictions prevailing in the society and the issues that would attract the masses to them rather than the Government. In an interview, CPI (Maoist) General Secretary Ganapathy told the Worker magazine in 2007, "Middle class is terribly affected by such issues as price rise, insecurity, corruption, unemployment for their children, high cost of education and healthcare, threats from real estate mafia etc. Keeping these in mind, our party has drawn up plans to mobilise the middle class into struggles on such issues."

These observations clearly indicate that the Government of India, irrespective of the parties in power, has often neglected the real problems of people, which has led to a situation when the people, especially those in the hinterlands, are getting distanced from the democratic system of which the true essence should be peace and welfare for all. Considering that the Maoist insurgents are fighting against the Government, it should be the first task of the Government to identify and address the problems so as to plug the voids that provide space for non-State actors to grow. At the same time, there are various sections that present the democratic picture of the country, if knit together properly. There are certain things that they also can do.

Fearing the expanse of the conclusion and suggestions part into a separate paper, the author here wants to make a few suggestions and urges the Government as well as various constituents of the society to think over it and come up with refinements with an aim to achieve the peaceful coexistence of all sections, and also achieve improvement in the current system of governance.

- As the Prime Minister Dr. Manmohan Singh has rightly pointed out, the approach to the Maoist violence should be a blend of firm but sophisticated handling of violence and sensitive handling of developmental aspects. Similar observation has been made by several other quarters. It will be a right choice if there is a wider participation of the society as well as the Government in not only planning but also implementing and sustaining developmental initiatives.
- Normally, the lack of employment leads to brewing of discontent, which gets refined into resistance against the Government. Hence, whenever a new project is coming up, the concerned business house should be asked to ensure

that people from the area where the project is coming up physically, should get direct or indirect jobs. For the purpose, there needs to be an effective policy with necessary penal and incentive provisions.

- Another issue that the Government needs to pay an urgent attention is the fear of displacement, especially among the tribals. The fear is a result of inadequate and ineffective implementation of relocation and rehabilitation scheme over the years in case of several projects. This has eroded trust in the Government as well as the machinery implementing development initiatives. To restore that, and thereby not allowing the non-State actors like Maoists to take advantage of the situation, serious thought needs to be given to having a mechanism to monitor effective and speedier implementation of relief and rehabilitation packages.
- As is the general experience, corruption has harmed interests of real beneficiaries of any relief package or scheme with a segmental focus. A tougher monitoring mechanism, faster institution and completion of enquiry, clubbed with deterrent punishment clause and speedier trial process is need of the hour. Corruption and pilferage free development could be achieved only then.
- To break the nexus between the Babus and Netas, corporate houses and babus, and a variety of other complex mutual beneficiaries, the Right to Information Act should be amended in such a manner as to empower the people to have better access to official records as well as to incorporate a deterrent punishment to the person, guided by ill motives, using details obtained under the Act for his/her individual gains.
- There is an urgent need to make the polity, judiciary, public administration, NGOs, police establishments, scientific and educational institutions, corporates accountable to public. Though there could be discretion, it should be defined and made known to public.
- Though the electoral reforms are taking place, there are still many loopholes that lead to creating a negative impression about the politicians and the Parliamentary system, which may end up in creating a negative impression about one's

own country. For instance, though there is a provision to disclose property details of the political leaders at the time of elections, there is no deterrent clause in case the information furnished is inadequate, incorrect, or false. That needs to be introduced, with a provision for disqualification, if the concerned candidate/political leader furnishes inadequate, incorrect or false information. This will be a step towards reaching the stage of probity in public life.

- Apart from expediting the process of electoral reforms, it is also necessary to carry out judicial, political, economic, and developmental reforms faster. While carrying out the process of reforms, there needs to be a mechanism for audit involving the public scrutiny part, to ensure proper implementation of these reforms and their consequent policy transformations.
- As the Maoists say, "The agrarian revolution is the basis that ensures unending flow of recruits into the people's army." Why has the situation in agriculture sector worsened to such a level? A thought must be given. It also warrants major policy intervention, not just occasional relief packages, as far as agriculture sector is concerned. For the purpose, remunerative prices and direct access of farmers to the consumers (not the markets) would do.
- FICCI Report on Security and Terrorism, 2009, makes an interesting observation: "In the conflict zones where the Maoists and security forces are repeatedly clashing, there are also evidence of many other parties creeping in -vested interests such as forest contractors, timber merchants, tendu leaf contractors, and investors who handle Maoist money in legal market, arms suppliers, foreign supporters, caste forces, criminals etc. The Government often overlooks many of these aspects." Such inputs need to be taken seriously not only from security point of view, but also from a view of deeper social analysis to understand the complex nature of several issues. With a clear analysis of the social situation emerging out from various security-related situations, the Government should formulate policies for different sectors, different regions, and even different classes. Given the diverse socio-cultural set up of India, it will indeed be a Herculean

task, but then, do simple solutions to complex problems emerge without understanding the complexities involved?

- Social security sector is a much neglected one. This picture should change to create an atmosphere of confidence among the people who are often bogged down by the financial insecurity aspect.
- As far as action against the Maoists goes, the Government needs to put in place a mechanism whereby only the ones deeply involved in the banned organisation are singled out. Else, as has been the case in many parts of the country, the cops perceive all critics of the Government as Maoist sympathisers or anti-nationals. If these critics are well-intentioned and want the Government to correct its course, careless police action would push them towards non-State anti-national actors.

Though the suggestions are mostly broader in nature, I sincerely hope that they would provide a general frame of measures to be taken to ensure that peace prevails in the society, with most of the sections in the society getting due attention and importance.

One must keep into mind that the Maoists grow into the cushion of contradictions in the society, and hence it becomes imperative for any Government or any right-thinking individual to try and remove the contradictions.

If the contradictions are not properly addressed, one can imagine a civil war like situation in the country, which would not benefit anybody. While the Maoists as well as the Government, both, appear to be following Lord Fisher's famous quote "The essence of war is violence. Moderation in war is imbecility", they are concentrating more on fighting each other than solving the problems haunting the people.

It is time all that all those who believe in violence must realise that there are no winners after violence, because the casualties complicate the matter further and lead to creating newer grounds for waging another war.

Let us not forget that it is better to have a constructive peace than the calm that prevails after destruction.

Table State-wise Extent of Naxal Violence During 2007 to 2011.

State	*2007*		*2008*		*2009*		*2010*		*2011*	
	Incidents	*Deaths*	*Incidents*	*Deaths*	*Incidents*	*Deaths*	*Incidents*	*Deaths*	*Incidents*	*Deaths*
Andhra Pradesh	138	45	92	46	66	18	100	24	54	9
Bihar	135	67	164	73	232	72	307	97	313	64
Chhattisgarh	582	369	620	242	529	290	625	343	458	202
Jharkhand	482	157	484	207	742	208	501	157	515	182
M.P	09	2	07	00	1	—	7	1	8	0
Maharashtra	94	25	68	22	154	93	94	45	109	54
Odisha	67	17	103	101	266	67	218	79	192	53
Uttar Pradesh	9	3	4	—	8	2	6	1	1	0
West Bengal	32	6	35	26	255	158	350	258	90	41
Others	17	5	14	4	5	—	5	0	5	1
TOTAL	**1565**	**696**	**1591**	**721**	**2258**	**908**	**2213**	**1005**	**1745**	**606**

Source: Ministry of Home Affairs, Government of India.

Table Comparative Important Parameters of Naxal Violence during 2007 to 2011

S. No	Parameters	2007	2008	2009	2010	2011
(A)	No. of incidents	1565	1591	2258	2213	1745
(B)	Civilians killed	460	490	591	720	464
	(Out of which 'Police informers' killed)		170	211	323	216
(C)	No. of Security Forces killed	236	231	317	285	142
(D)	No. of encounters with police	276	271	309	272	223
(E)	No. of attacks on police (including landmines)	182	192	250	230	131
(F)	No. of naxalites killed (during encounters as well as attacks on police	141	199	219	172	99
(G)	No. of naxalites arrested	1456	1743	1981	2916	1972
(H)	No. of naxalites surrendered	390	400	150	266	393
(I)	Total no. of arms snatched	233	1219	217	256	67
(J)	Total no. of arms recovered	352	1511	572	642	624
(K)	Arms training camps held	48	52	61	94	84
(L)	No. of Jan Adalats held	68	71	50	75	96

Source: Ministry of Home Affairs, Government of India.

Table State-wise Statistics of Various Indies of Naxal Violence for 2011 vis-a-vis 2010.

Sl. No.	State	No. of incidents	No. of civilians killed	No. of Security Forces killed	No. of encounters with police	No. of attacks on police (including landmines)	No. of naxalites killed (encounters and attacks)	No. of naxalites arrested	No. of naxalites surrendered	Total no of arms snatched	Total no. of arms recovered held	Arms training camps held	No. of Jan Adalats
		A	B	C	D	E	F	G	H	I	J	K	L
1.	Andhra Pradesh	54 (100)	9 (24)	0 (0)	6 (14)	1 (2)	4 (13)	150 (289)	242 (141)	0 (0)	24 (48)	0 (0)	8 (3)
2.	Bihar	313 (307)	61 (72)	3 (25)	17 (20)	13 (24)	14 (5)	426 (364)	26 (13)	4 (61)	159 (59)	12 (1)	16 (18)
3.	Chhattisgarh	458 (625)	122 (171)	80 (172)	99 (126)	75 (125)	34 (83)	504 (902)	20 (6)	29 (109)	108 (122)	24 (57)	13 (14)
4.	Jharkhand	515 (501)	149 (132)	33 (25)	42 (57)	23 (26)	16 (15)	377 (359)	17 (23)	17 (15)	165 (217)	24 (9)	54 (26)
5.	Maharashtra	109 (94)	44 (35)	10 (10)	20 (7)	7 (14)	3 (3)	92 (76)	15 (22)	1 (0)	12 (27)	7 (4)	1 (0)
6.	M.P	8 (7)	0 (0)	0 (1)	0 (1)	0 (0)	0 (0)	6 (0)	0 (2)	1 (1)	12 (1)	0 (0)	0 (0)
7.	Odisha	192 (218)	39 (62)	14 (17)	21 (10)	9 (21)	23 (10)	148 (247)	49 (48)	10 (4)	68 (32)	7 (10)	3 (100)
7.	Uttar Pradesh	1 (6)	0 (1)	0 (0)	0 (2)	0 (0)	0 (0)	13 (77)	9 (1)	0 (0)	2 (26)	0 (0)	0 (0)
8.	West Bengal	90 (350)	39 (223)	2 (35)	18 (34)	2 (16)	5 (42)	223 (536)	15 (6)	0 (63)	74 (110)	10 (12)	1 (4)
10.	Others	5 (5)	1 (0)	0 (0)	0 (1)	1 (2)	0 (0)	33 (66)	0 (4)	5 (3)	0 (0)	0 (1)	0 (0)
	Total	**1745 (2213)**	**464 (720)**	**142 (285)**	**223 (272)**	**131 (230)**	**99 (172)**	**1972 (2916)**	**393 (266)**	**67 (256)**	**624 (642)**	**84 (94)**	**96 (75)**

Source: Ministry of Home Affairs, Government of India.

9

Politics of Terror and Contemporary Times

Ram Puniyani

Introduction

Today modern society is full of insane acts of terror. All over the globe, acts of violence by political groups seeking justice or revenge are dime a dozen. September 11, 2001 brought to fore the most dreaded phenomenon and global attention has been glued to this phenomenon. In this attack over three thousand innocent people died. Later many a terror attacks were witnessed in Pakistan, Afghanistan and other parts of world. Not a month passes when one does not hear about the death of innocents in one more such act in one or the other corner of the globe.

India has been tragically witnessing many acts of terror. "These acts have been occurring since last two decades. There is a long lists of these tragic acts but some of these which have tormented the society and are permanently etched in our memory. For example, March 1993: Mumbai serial bombings, which killed 257 people and injured more than 1,100, December 13th2001where more than a dozen people, including five gunmen, killed in an attack on parliament in New Delhi. May 14, 2002 Militants attack an army camp near Kashmir's winter capital, Jammu, killing more than 30, including wives and children of soldiers. September 24, 2002, Militants with guns and explosives attack the Akshardham Hindu temple in the Western state of Gujarat, 31 killed, more than 80 injured. August 2003, two taxis packed with explosives blow up outside a Mumbai tourist attraction and a busy market, killed 52 and wounded more than 100. In October 2005, three bombs planted in busy New Delhi market and killed 62 people and injured hundreds. In March 2006, twin bombings at a railway station and Sankatmochan temple in Varanasi killed 20 people.

There are some more tragic acts, for example, July 2006: Seven bombs on Mumbai's train killed over 200 and injure 700 others, September 8, 2006: 30 people were killed and 100 hurt in twin blasts at a mosque in Malegaon, February 19, 2007: Two bombs explode aboard a train bound from India to Pakistan, Samjhauta Express, burning to death at least 66 passengers, most of them Pakistanis, May 18, 2007: A bomb exploded during Friday prayers at a historic mosque, Mecca Masjid Hyderabad, killed 14. Police later shoot dead five people in clashes with hundreds of enraged Muslims who protest against the attack, August 25, 2007: Three explosions within minutes at an amusement park and a street-side food stall in Hyderabad killed 40 people, May 13, 2008: Seven blasts strike Jaipur and killed 63 people and wounded hundreds of people, July 25, 2008: Nine explosions in Bangalore created terror that killed two people and injured twelve. July 26, 2008: 21 blasts hit Ahmedabad and killed 55 and injured 100, September 13, 2008: Five blasts rock busy markets of New Delhi and killed 25 and injured over 100. And three live bombs were defused in India Gate, Regal Cinema and Central Park.

Because of these tragic attacks, huge forces were deployed at airports to check and cross check the people travelling. People have become used to being frisked, searched during such travels. Muslims have bore the biggest brunt of these searches. Just being Muslim is enough cause for someone to be thoroughly probed and searched. In the wake of Mumbai blasts wholesale arrest of Muslim youths has been the norm with the police, on the pretext that they must be harboring terrorists or they must be having sympathies with the terrorists since they are Muslims. The social life is getting affected. The orthodoxy and right wing religio-political streams are coming to the fore in very aggressive and assertive manner. The atmosphere has become full of suspicion. To worsen the matter there is a section of global and local media playing on this sentiment to widen the divide between different religious communities. There are sectarian groups, wearing different garbs, who are having a field day in reaping the harvest of hate.

Defining Terrorism

Defining terrorism is not very simple, various interpretations and definitions have come up. The states have focused on talking of terrorist acts, violence; death of innocents in this process. As such in popular parlance, in some regions, in some circles these acts of terror are legitimised as an act of political campaign. LTTE, ULFA, who are labeled as terrorists are looked up as freedom fighters amongst a section. As such terrorism can be understood "as an act of violence against unarmed civilians as a means of bargaining politically over specific demands or making a general statement." (Hensman, 2002: 29) Further Hensman adds very aptly, "It should be irrelevant whether the perpetrators are state parties or non state parties, and other characteristics (like skin colour, ethnicity, gender, religion, nationality, sexual orientation, disability, social origin and anything else) of the perpetrators or the victims should likewise be irrelevant. (Hensman 2002: 156) While such groups have wreaked havoc, even the elected governments have also resorted to this violence. "Statist definitions (of terrorism) portray terrorism to cover sedition, conspiracy, killing, murder, arson, explosions and public disorder to undermine the state..., twist due process of an evidentiary norms against the individual and prescribe heavy punishment ... political terrorism abjures the state's definition and seeks to define terrorism as political freedom struggle to support the claims of justice and self determination with no holds barred."(Dhavan, Times of India, August 23) Accordingly state governments formulate harsh laws and try to go overboard in their response to the extent of punishing the innocents in the process and so the "War on Terror", POTA, armed forces acts. Dhavan further adds, "A people's definition of terrorism draws from the experience of civilian populations. Post World War II, terrorism against the people acquired a new dimension when America bombed Hiroshima and Nagasaki in 1945 and later carpet bombed Vietnam with Napalm". The experience of Afghanistan and Iraq is no different, neither the one of Israel's attack on Lebanon.

Islam, Muslims and Terrorism

Since the 11th September 2001, attack on WTC, the word 'Islamic Terrorism' started being popularised and by now it has become part of social common sense. "In India, the Kashmir militancy indulged in by a section of youth is again cited as example of Muslim terrorists. To add to this the incidents of Akshardham temple, 26/11, 2008 Mumbai attack, Ansal Plaza, high jacking of Indian Airlines plane to Kandhar, attack on parliament are blown up as, in all these either Muslims were involved or in some cases it was projected that they were. Some of these reports had serious holes in the story presented by the authorities, but since there can be no ratification by citizens committees it is difficult to doubt or believe in some of these." (Puniyani, 2010: 15) All said and done, there are enough number of cases where Muslims are involved and organisations like Al Qaeda, Lashkar-e-Tayyba, Hamas have become household names. But interestingly there are many other organisations using violence which are not much taken note of much.

Terrorists as such have come from many religions. But they have not resorted to this path due to religion. One of the major such organisations was Liberation Tiger of Tamil Elam (LTTE), the majority of the members of this are Hindus. One member of this group, Dhanu strapped a bomb and killed Rajiv Gandhi. Similarly Khalistani movement was the major force resorting to terror in 1990s. Those belonging to Christian and Hindu militants are active in North East India. Worldwide, the Irish Republican Army militants belong to Christianity, the one who bombed a Hotel in Cairo in 1942 was a Jew, and the Oklahoma bomber was a Christian. Over 80 youth campers were killed in a shoting spree by Anders Behring Breivik. (http://articles.nydailynews.com/2011-07-24/news/29827213_1_summer-camp-cold-blooded-killer-shot) Wherever dissatisfaction goes beyond a particular level, some of the people do resort to violence to achieve their supposed goal. It is not related to any one religion in particular. All Tripura Tiger Force, Japanese Red Army, Lords Salvation Army and ETA are some more examples of organisations, which are scattered in different parts of world, using terror tactics for their political goals and have nothing to do with Islam.

During last decade and a half, Islam has been projected to be violent. The media and many a state apparatus have on purpose projected this image of Islam. As such Muslims are no uniform community. The basic assumption which comes from this formulation is that religion is the cause of terrorism. On the contrary, terrorism is a phenomenon, which comes into being due to social political and economic circumstances. Religion is used as a cover for the terrorist activities. The identity of terrorists is not always derived from and is not always around religion. As such Khalistanis derived their identity from Sikhism. The alleged Muslim terrorists had multiple identities; the ones in Palestine, from where terrorism began had Palestinian identity, in Kashmir it began as Kashmiriayat. The Islamic identity with this sort of terrorism came more particularly with AL Qaeda, which was set up by the CIA, the US through ISI of Pakistan to fight against the USSR armies in Afghanistan.

Terrorism and Religion's identity

It is true that some of the terrorists are showing the Islamic identity but that's not true all through. Even with this large spectrum of Islamic identity, the ones' trained by CIA wore this identity prominently on their sleeves and they tried to present as if they are doing Jihad, they were killing the kafirs. As such they were indoctrinated in the madrasas especially set up for this purpose by CIA. These Madrassas were set up under the Kissinger doctrine of 'Asians should be made to fight Asians'. It was formulated in the madrasas as that the Communists are kafirs since they don't believe in Allah, killing them is a jihad and those dying in this jihad will go to jannat, where 72 virgins are waiting for them. The US concoction of establishment of madrasas had strong impact on the Muslim youth who came in to get training in these with the readiness to lay down their lives for the US goal of occupying Afghanistan in the long run. (http://www.informationclearinghouse.info/article9561.htm) As such what is called as Islamic identity of terrorists, only those trained in madrasas set up by CIA-ISI nexus, use the Islamic identity. In this also Jehad and Kafir are used in the main.

The Madrassas set up by US-CIA-ISI was a very clever manipulation of the words like Jihad and Kafir in particular. As we know, the historical meaning of these terms was much different in the beginning. Also there are many an interpretation to these words. The media and many a state apparatus have on purpose projected this image of Islam as being associated with terrorism. Muslims are no uniform community. And there are different interpretations of Islam. The media highlights any sensational violent act and ignores the pacifist ones'. Comments of fanatics are projected prominently as the Islamic voice. The sober and moderate statements are either ignored or find their place in some small corner of the media.

The misuse of the word Jihad by fanatics adds to the problem. Any act of Muslim terrorists is supposed to be a Jihad, as some of them project it in the same manner. Asghar Ali Engineer, one of the liberal interpreters of Islam states, "It is Jihad, which is one of the pillars of Islam precisely because it does not necessarily mean war. Jihad ... means utmost effort, not violence and it is obligatory on Muslims to make utmost efforts (in wisely manner) to spread the message of Allah so as to create a just and compassionate society. This is what is obligatory, not waging a war at all. Prophet himself has exemplified it on many occasions especially at the time of Slh-I-Hudabiya (i.e., peace of Hudaibiyah and Fath-I-Mecca)." (Engineer, Institute of Islamic Studies. Oct. 98)

As for radical Islamist groups, Jihad is being used as a cynical ruse to whip up religious fervour for their cause. "Historically, Jihad was used rhetorically by the imperialist powers to justify their worldly expansionist designs. In its original sense, jihad was more of an inner moral cleansing for the community. This was called Jehad-e-Akbar (The Great Jihad). But now, the whole notion of Jihad is being used as an instrument for legitimizing militaristic, monarchic and dictatorial regimes. As for these radical Islamist groups, jihad is being used as a cynical ruse to whip up religious fervour for their cause."(Mushirul Hasan, Interview, Tehelka.com)

Arundhati Roy says that "In 1979 after the Soviet invasion of Afghanistan, the CIA and Pakistan ISI (Inter Service Intelligence) launched the largest covert operation in the history of CIA. Their purpose was to harness the energy of Afghan residence to the Soviets and expand it into a holy war, an Islamic Jihad, which would turn the Muslim Countries within the Soviet zone of influence, against the communist regime and to eventually destabilise it. When it began it was meant to be Soviet Union's Vietnam. It turned out to be much larger than that. Over the years CIA funded and recruited 1,00,000 radical Mujahidin from 40 Islamic countries as soldiers for American proxy war. (In Afghanistan" Arundhati Roy, The Algebra of Infinite Justice)

It is true that some fanatical Muslims found on the fringe, use certain medieval interpretation and usage as eternally binding and believe that Kafirs should be slayed (killed). Also those hostile to Islam use this term to show the intolerance of Islam.

War on Terror or Hunting for Oil

'War on Terror' is a euphemism for the US aims to take political and military control of different areas of the World, either for acquisition of oil wealth or for military goals. The acts of terror by the groups scattered here and there are no uniform entity, which can be subject to aggression and eliminated. Since they are scattered and are faceless, it is difficult to identify them and restrain them. In the process what happens is that US and its allies have been picking one after the other areas and bombing them into deserts. The civilian population, the non combatants are the biggest victim of the same. Operation Iraqi freedom was launched after the pretexts of 'Weapons of Mass Destruction' failed miserably. UN observer recommendations were bypassed and a war was launched, which has met massive resistance from the people of Iraq. It is a war against Iraqi people and incidents like Abu Ghraib prison, where the prisoners were stripped naked and asked to make human pyramid, and butchering on the Iraqi streets has been made the norm by the US army. This army by now is desperate and all the attempts by US to outsource the war and to rope in the soldiers of poorer nations has not met with any success, as the US aim of offering people of poor countries as sacrifices goats here failed. Even the US army is comprised mainly of the underprivileged sections of US population.

The lack of any credible reason for attacking Afghanistan led many an observer to comment that, ". . . the war against Afghans was very much in line with the US's historical role in Afghanistan. In 1970s, the US hired seven different parties of fundamentalists called Mujahidin. These were extremists hired by the CIA during the cold war 'to draw the Soviets in to Afghan trap" as later revealed by former National Security Advisor, Zbignew Brezinsky. The CIA gave arms and ammunition to Mujahidin.... Using these weapons and sophisticated training in the art of terror, these men successfully drove out the Soviets, but also waged terrible war on their own people killing at least 45000 people in Kabul alone. (Ninan Koshy, WOT, p. 62 –63)

As the invasion of Afghanistan began just within few weeks, the US claim that they prepared for this in three weeks time is to be taken with a pinch of salt. "Credible reports have appeared that the US was planning to take military action against Afghanistan to oust Taliban months before September 11."(Koshy p. 63) To train Al-Qaeda US had spent over 80000 million dollars and also provided 7000 tons of armaments, including the stringer missiles.

The US propaganda machine, keeps dishing out different slogans to serve its foreign policy. In cold war era it was defence of freedom, now it is war on terror. The US media and other media world over following the trails of US, toe the same line.

International Tribunal on War Crimes against Afghanistan and Iraq held United States and its President George W. Bush responsible for the crimes which took place in the region. It held that US has been the criminal of aggression and consequent crimes.

((http://www.mindfully.org/Reform/2004/Afghanistan-Criminal-Tribunal10mar04.htm)

The Jury of Conscience in its report released in Istambul on 27 June, 2005 opined that "this war (on Iraq) as one of the most unjust in history: 'The Bush and Blair administrations blatantly ignored the massive opposition to the war expressed by millions of people around the world. They embarked upon one of the most unjust, immoral, and cowardly wars in history. The Anglo-American occupation of Iraq of the last 27 months has led to the destruction and devastation of the Iraqi state and society. Law and order have broken down completely, resulting in a pervasive lack of human security; the physical infrastructure is in shambles; the health care delivery system is a mess; the education system has ceased to function; there is massive environmental and ecological devastation; and, the cultural and archeological heritage of the Iraqi people has been desecrated.' (http://www.worldtribunal.org/main/?b=93)

Religion and Violence

Islamism can, indeed, not be reduced to religious fervour or to extreme moral rigorism characteristic of the Taliban or be reduced to the recourse to violence. It is defined essentially, in its relationship to politics and hence to the state, by its efforts towards realisation of a truly Muslim society. In Islamism the conquest of political power is justified by the will to impose the Sharia, the sole juridical basis of social relationships before which no other non-Islamic law can exist. Asghar Ali Engineer a noted Islamic scholar, who has interpreted Islam in a liberal manner, points out, 'The concept of Jihad in Islam has been grossly misunderstood by Muslims and non-Muslims. It is thought that Islam encourages violence and force and that Allah wants to spread Islam with sword or at the point of gun. The acts of some Muslim extremists and terrorists provide proof for this violent image of Islam. . . .Truth is quite otherwise" (Islam and Modern Age, Vol. I, 1998, Mumbai).

Asghar Ali Engineer further points out, 'there is no question of force or violence in spreading Islam. This was popularised by the West after the crusades, which again had nothing to do with spread of religion. It was, in fact the wars of territorial conquest. As far as the spread of religion is concerned Quran rules out violence completely through number of pronouncements. It very forcefully states, la ikrah fi'al-din (there is no compulsion in religion (Asghar Ali Engineer 2: 256). Also it makes it plain that one can invite to the path of Allah through wisdom and godly manner (Asghar Ali Engineer 16: 125). It is no less important that Quran accepted the truth brought by Prophets before Muhammad. (Asghar Ali Engineer, Ibid)

The Khalistani movement was also fundamentalist in nature. It remained only a movement of rebellion and did not achieve power to exercise its control on the weaker sections. Hindutva had come up in response to the rising secular movement of Indian National

Congress. It did not grow to threaten democracy in India. But the during last two decades it has assumed menacing proportions due to the rise in the number of middle classes, (Rich peasants, rich professionals, petty industrialists etc.) It also derives its legitimacy from a particular version of Hinduism (Brahminical) and is repressive to Women and Dalits. The Islamic terrorists harbor the same values i.e. being repressive towards weaker section. This use of Religion for retrograde politics, which is against the Human rights of weaker sections of society, cuts across different religions.

Malegaon Blast

A blast occurred in Malegaon in the Kabristan, which is near a mosque. It was Friday, 8th September 2008, at 1.15 pm, just after the prayers. This was a Shab-e-Barat holiday and there was bigger crowd. In this blast 37 people died and 125 got injured. Most of the people who died were Muslim pilgrims. The police investigators blamed SIMI for the blast. One person Noor Ul-Hooda was blamed to be a part of SIMI, and he was arrested for the act of terror. Others suspects were Shabbir Batterywala of Lashkar-e-Tayyaba, and Raees Ahmad were arrested as co conspirator. While there was a murmur that Hindutva organisations may be involved, the authorities ruled it out on the ground that the type of explosives, RDX, are not available with Bajrang Dal etc., and that the type of bomb used in Malegaon was too sophisticated for Bajrang Dal type organisation. They do not have such organisational capability. While police pointed out that the pattern of these blasts is similar to the one which occurred in other mosques in Maharashtra, still Bajrang Dal was not suspected. From the accused confessions were elicited under coercion, they denied the charges in front of magistrates and no further headway could be made, there was no concrete proof.

In same Malegaon, another blast took place two years later. The low intensity blast took place in the crowded Bhikku Chowk in Malegaon, at a time when people were breaking their Ramzan fast. Initially police thought that it is blast of gas cylinder but later confirmed that the blast took place due to the device tied to the Hero Honda motorcycle. This investigation was conducted by Hemant Karkare of Maharastra ATS, who was later killed in the Mumbai

27/11 attack. The investigation led to Sadhvi Prgaya Singh Thakur, Swami Dayanand Pandey, serving army officer Lt Col. Prasad Shrikant Purohit and retired army officer Maj. Upadhyay. They are behind the bars. Subhash Gatade said that it could not rule out the possibility of Hindu extremist hand in Monday's blast in Malegaon. The ATS is planning to question the activists of Hindu Janjagruti Samiti, Sanatan Sanstha and other stray Hindu extremist organisations for their possible involvement in the act. (Malegaon, Modassa and Mehrauli Blasts, Subhash Gatade, in Malegaon to Ajmer -All India Secular Forum 2010: 34)

Mecca Masjid Blast and Investigation

Mecca Mosque blast in Hyderabad occurred on May 18th 2007, at the time of Namaz prayers in the afternoon. At that time, thousands of people were inside the mosque. Further, police as usual put the fingers at Harkat-ul-Jihad-al-Islami or HUJI and the Students' Islamic Movement of India (SIMI) as the main suspects behind the Friday Mecca mosque blast. Nearly 25 Muslim youth were arrested alleging different affiliations, but all of them were released after six months, for the lack of evidence. In both Malegaon and Hyderabad Mecca Masjid, like many other places, what is evident is that Muslims had been the main victims and later the main suspects, showing the track followed by the officials that all terrorists are Muslims, which has been the their line of thinking in all cases of blasts.

For India investigating authorities of all types, after every act of blast, the foreign link (i.e., Pakistan) Harkat-ul-Jihad, Lashkar-e-Tayyba, Mujahidin etc., is the first suspicion. Many youths are arrested under the label as the old member of SIMI, as SIMI was banned in 2001. It became a matter of routine after every blast, Malegaon; Mecca Masjid in Hyderabad, Jaipur and other places was broken with the impeccable proof of Sadhvi Pragya Singh Thakur's motor cycle being found in Malegaon. The trace of motorcycle link led to Swami Dayanand Pandey, Lt Col Shrikant Purohit and many other associates. Society has witnessed that after most of the blasts so far, Muslim youth were arrested on the charge of being behind the blasts, were harassed for months and then released for the lack of evidence. This was more or less a routine pattern and it frightened the whole Muslim community to no end.

Many a Muslim youths' careers were crushed due to these reckless and baseless arrests. Many a minority families underwent severe problems, were ostracised from their own community once they were dragged into the net on the charges which were guided more by the prevalent biases or stereotypes than any substance. SIMI came to be regarded as the core organisation responsible for fomenting trouble through youth. Despite the ban on SIMI in 2001, the Muslim youth kept on being labeled as SIMI activists and were put behind the bar.

With the World scenario tilting against the Islam and Muslims, courtesy the radical Islamists trained in the Madrassas set up in Pakistan with US aid, the popular psyche perceived an average Muslim as a terrorist and police machinery operated on this understanding. Even when scores of lives were shattered and the community came under the intimidation of highest order, the Government did not put any corrective to this pattern of investigation with which police was pursuing its work. The Hindutva groups came under the scanner with the Nanded bomb blast in the house of Bajrang Dal Workers who were making bombs. (http://www.news24online.com/Hindutva-terror-is-making-its-presence-felt-Book_News24_34868.aspx)

1. On 6th April 2006 two Bajrang Dal workers died when making the bombs. The place where they died belonged to the RSS worker and saffron flag was hoisted atop the hose. There was also a board of Bajrang Dal Nanded Branch on the wall of the house.
2. In Thane on 4th June 2008, two Hindu Jagran Samiti workers were arrested for planting the bombs in the basement of Gadkari Rangayatan, due to which 7 people got injured. The same group was involved in the blasts in Vashi, Panvel also.
3. In Goa a bomb kept in a scooter went off on the eve of Diwali (17th October 2009) in Margao. It killed Malgonda Patil and seriously injured Yogesh Naik. Another bomb was detected in Sancoale in a truck carrying 40 youth for Narkasur competition. Both the activists belonged to Sanatan Sanstha. The second aim of this blast was to create communal tension in Margao, which has a history of communal violence. This group takes inspiration from Savarkar (Hindu Mahasabha)

and Hedgewar (RSS) and indoctrinates its members into hating Christians and Muslims.

4. On 24th August 2008 two Bajrang Dal activists died in Kanpur, while making bombs. The Kanpur zone IGP S.N. Singh stated that their investigations have revealed that this group was planning massive explosions all over the state.
5. Indian Express, 23 Oct. 2008 reports that those involved in the bomb blast in Malegaon and Modasa (September. 2008) had links with Akhil Bhartiya Vidyarthi Parishad.

Similarly in Tenkasi, Tamil Nadu pipe bomb there was another attack on RSS office on January 2008 and it was projected to have been done by Jehadi Muslims. The investigation revealed many a Hindu names and later the investigations was frozen. In an alleged Fidayin attack was claimed that in the attack on RSS office in Nagpur (June 1, 2006) three of them were killed in the police encounter, as per the police version. Citizens Inquiry report, headed by Justice Kolse Patil doubted the police version in a serious way; the clarifications did not come through from the authorities.

By now a pattern is emerging where not only that Bajrang Dal activists are carrying guns and swords in the public display of the arms, but also are active in undertaking the acts of terror. It is likely that in many cases their role has remained uninvestigated. There is a deliberate cover up of these incidents. Some of these leads are not being pursued while the police are hyper active in cases where suspected Muslim youth seem to be involved, and that too just on the basis of their confessions. This is a biased attitude of the authorities involved.

A tribunal was organised by Anhad and associated human rights organisations in Hyderabad in 2007. (http://www.anhadin.net/article37.html) It had a very demanding task of hearing and going to the truth of the various alleged culprits. What was surprising was the gross violation of laws which the police indulged in freely? Not only that alleged culprits were kept in custody and denied all their rights, their relatives were not informed, their date of arrest was shown to be much later than the real time they were picked up. The torture which they were subjected to is beyond words, the wrecking of poor families which took place due to the whole process is shattering. The careers of many a promising young men was totally ruined due to such arrests without any proof what so ever. Is all this reflective of the poor norms, poor professional training of the officers? Is it rank inefficiency couched in this cruelty or the tormentors are acting like this due to the prevalent biases which have gone deep into the whole society including these officers?

The pattern observed in most of the cases was that there were illegal detentions.

What happens to the future of those who are accused and released later? The students lose their career-track, at times colleges don't take them back until court ruling is brought to that effect. The families of accused get ostracised from the community out of fear. Others stop relating to them. The business gets a severe set back and at these times banks refuse to give them loans etc. Some of the accused are also tempted to become approvers with the carrot dangled in front of them that they will be released. The powers vested with the police seem to be present only through their misuse, most of the times.

A two way impression operates in the society. One, amongst the larger sections of society, the Muslim terrorists is taken as a big threat to the nation. Two, amongst Muslims, there is feeling is that state is totally partisan and deliberate injustice is being done to them since they are Muslims.

In Malegaon blast, Maharashtra ATS chief Hemant Karkare meticulously shown having connection of Sadhvi Pragya Singh Thakur and many others from the Hidutva combine, associated with one or the other offshoot of RSS or inspired by the RSS ideology of Hindu nation, trained in the communal ideology of looking at people through the prism of their religion, and religion alone. (http://www.dnaindia.com/india/report_hemant-karkare-feared-for-his-safety-from-hindu-extremists-digvijay-singh_1479752) Karkare's efforts brought out enough skeletons from the cupboard of Hindutva stable and somewhere the stubborn police and the political authorities also started looking the other way leading to the plethora of organisations, broadly known as Sangh parivar. It is also a matter of great concern that same Hemant Karkare started being abused by Hindutva elements, intimidation and threat to his life began. Incidentally Karkare was killed on the fateful night of 26/11 Mumbai terror attack.

Conclusion

Terrorism is a phenomenon, which has come up in the guise of religion. It has nothing to do with religion. At global level it is the US lust for oil, which laid the foundation of Al Qaeda, Taliban and their horrific acts of terror. In India the Hindutva groups have resorted to terror as a pretext to avenge the acts of terror by Muslim groups and also to lay the foundation of Hindu Rashtra. Both these are creating havoc in the life of the society and killing the innocents.

References

Asghar Ali. Engineer, Islam and Modern Age, Vol. I, 1998, Mumbai.

Asghar Ali Engineer, Islam and the concept of Jihad, Institute of Islamic Studies, Vol. 1, Oct 1998.

Asghar Ali Engineer-Concept of Islamic State, Aman, April-May 99.

Dhavan, Rajeev, Get the Guilty, Times of India, August 23.

Grare, F. Manohar, New Delhi, 2001.

Hasan, Mushirul, (Interview, www.tehelka.com).

Hensman, Rohini, Terrorism, Imperialism and War, Build Mumbai 2002, p. 29.

Khalid Durran, The Globalisation of Terrorism, In Review, Fall 2000.

Imam Raghib Asfahani Mufradat al-Qur'an, pp. 916-17, Lahore, 1971.

Suri, Sanjay. The Great Britain Bust, Outlook 28th August 2006.

Puniyani, Ram, Communal Politics, Sage Delhi 2002.

Puniyani, Ram, Terrorism, Imperialism and War, Build Mumbai 2002.

Puniyani Ram, Hashmi Shabnam (Editor), Mumbai Post 26/11, Sage, Delhi 2009.

Puniyani Ram, Terrorism: Oerceptions versus Relity, Mythri, Trivandrum, 2010, p. 15

Bibliography

Ahmad, Ajiaz, On Communalism and Globalisation: Offensives of the Far Right, Three Essays.

Ahmad, Aijaz, Iraq, Afghanistan and the Imperialism of Our Time, Delhi: Left Word Books, 2004.

Ali, Tariq, The Clash of Fundamentalism: Crusades, Jihads and Modernity, Delhi: Rupa Co., 2002, Pages: 428.

Armstrong, Karen, Islam: A Short History, Phoenix Press London.

Gatade Subhash, Godse's Children, Pharos Media, Delhi 2011.

Koshy, Ninan, WAR ON TERROR: Reordering the world, Leftward, p. 146, Delhi.

Maley, William, Afghanistan and the Taliban: The Rebirth of Fundamentalism? Delhi: Penguin Books India, 2001, p. 253.

Mamdani, Mahmood, Good Muslim Bad Muslim, Orient Longman, Hydrabad, 2003.

Puniyani, Ram, TERRORISM IMPERIALISM and WAR, Mumbai, BUILD, Mumbai, p. 227.

Prashad, Vijay, War against the Planet: The Fifth Afghan War, Imperialism, and Other Assorted Fundamentalisms, Delhi: Left Word Books, 2002, Pages: 110. Price: Rs. 75.

Imam, Zafar, Iraq-2003: The Return of Imperialism, Delhi: Aakar Books, 2004, Pages: 112.

Said, Edward W. The End of the Peace Process: Oslo and After, New York: Vintage Books, 2000, 389.

10

Communal Riots 2011

Asghar Ali Engineer

Riot free India still remains a distant dream. Like every year this year too i.e., 2010 several communal riots took place though earlier months did not witness violence and it appeared 2011 may be communally less violent. But during the middle and end of the year frequent riots took place once again shaming India. However, one can, on positive side, say that riots like Mumbai riots of 1992–93 and Gujarat like riots of 2002 have not taken place. But there is reason for this. The Shiv Sena or BJP, even if they want, cannot organise riots on such major scale. It needs highly emotional and surcharged atmosphere which cannot be generated so easily. It can be generated around some major event like demolition of Babri Masjid or some such major event.

The account was opened in Umarkhedi, Yewatmahal district in Maharashtra on 13th January when some Hindu boys indulged in eve-teasing of a Muslims girl and stone throwing started on both sides and people started running leaving their shoes and chappals fearing major outbreak of violence. But the police officer Mr. Deokatte controlled the violence effectively and called for reinforcements from district place.

It shows that if police is impartial it can control violence effectively and second thing that on ordinary things like eve-teasing an incident becomes a communal issue instead of mere law and order issue. On such things we get divided into Hindus and Muslims. Even if cricket ball hit someone we get communally divided or some accident takes place we communalise it. It is all result of constant communal propaganda going on by communal forces and the way our education system shapes our minds.

On 7th February there arose some dispute between a Christian Father and a rickshaw driver and strangely it assumed communal colour between Hindus and Muslims. Some communal elements gave it a Hindu-Muslim colour and entered into a Muslim Mohallah and pelted stones in which 10 persons were injured and they also set several houses and shops to fire and several vehicles were also burnt. This mob did not spare even tribals in the area. But unfortunately the police played a partial role and lathicharged Muslims and Adivasis only. Muslim properties were mostly targeted.

Baroda in Gujarat, another extremely communally sensitive area, witnessed communal violence on 16th February when some mischievous elements attacked a gate erected for celebrating Eid and burnt it. Several vehicles were also burnt down. One Chamis Kahar from fisher community was arrested. Kahars and Muslims often clash in Baroda as some Kahars and some Muslims are in illegal liquor business. A major riot had taken place between Kahars led by Shiva Kahar and Muslims in 1982 in Baroda.

On Monday i.e., 2nd March some communal elements in Sewri are of Mumbai tried to tear flags and posters put up on the occasion of Prophet's birthday and situation had become tense in the area. On 5th March after someone pushed a child the situation took a violent turn and stoning began from both sides. Some people even molested Muslim women. The police again alleged to have played partisan role and instead of taking action against the mischievous elements Lathi charged Muslims and arrested many young Muslims. According to the Police Commissioner communal colour was given to these incidents and he brought about re-conciliation between the two groups.

Next incident took place in Aurangabad, another communally sensitive area of Maharashtra. It happened on 20th March when some Muslims boys and girls were returning from S.B. College after appearing for accounts paper. The Muslims girls were wearing veil and despite this some communal elements threw colour on them and when they resisted they took out knives and Guptis and attacked them. Four students were seriously injured

The police arrested the attackers including those who had run away from the scene and Vice Chancellor Prof Pande of Dr. Ambedkar Marathwada University took prompt action against the administration of S.B. College who had refused to take any action against the attackers who were communally motivated.

On 6th April there were communal clashes between Hindus and Muslims in Dharavi, the Asia's largest slum area in Mumbai which is very sensitive and had witnessed large number of deaths in communal clashes in 1992–93 and subsequently Mohallah committees were formed to bring about peace in the area. On this occasion 4 persons were injured. The Peace committee had done commendable work in Dharavi and it was after a long time that communal clashes occurred here. The Peace Committee is no more active.

Maharashtra state unfortunately is communally quite sensitive and large number of communal clashes take place in this state every year. And in Maharashtra Mumbai and its suburbs are more sensitive. Maharashtra witnessed largest number of riots in last decade i.e., from 2001 to 2011. In all 1,192 riots took place in Maharashtra, the highest in India in which 172 persons were killed whereas in U.P. in all 1,112 communal incidents took place in which 384 persons were killed.

In Meerut communal violence broke out on 25th April, strangely enough, on a glass of cold water. It all happened in Qazipur village near Meerut on Sunday the 25th April when 3 persons from the village came to Choti Masjid and asked for water. When they were offered tap water they insisted on cold water and on being said there was no cold water the men became violent and beat up the person who offered tap water and also Imam of the mosque and some children studying there. They went to police station to complain but police did not take action. Many Muslims gathered outside the police station and began stoning in which city magistrate and some police officers were injured.

The crowd now attacked shops and houses. The crowd set fire to many police chowkies also. As a precautionary measure the police had to order all government and private schools to remain closed. And all this on a glass of cold water. Meerut is also a communally sensitive area and had witnessed horrible communal violence in 1987 in which PAC (Provincial Armed Constabulary) had pulled out 54 innocent Muslim youth from their houses and shot them dead and threw their dead bodies in Hindon Canal.

Next incident also occurred in U.P. in Moradabad. Some policemen entered into a Muslim house looking for one accused and not finding him there misbehaved with women of the house and seized Qur'an from the hands of Nurjahan, a 10 year old girl and turned the bed on which she was sitting thus throwing away Qur'an. This enraged Muslims as it implied dishonoring the Qur'an and the provoked crowd of Muslims began demanding action against the policeman concerned before dispersing.

Police kept on asking them to disperse and Muslims crowd kept on demanding action against the policemen and they also attacked the police thana and set fire to police vehicles and began stoning policemen. This of course enraged policemen and they began beating Muslims and also fired in which two Muslim men and one Hindu, an employee of petrol pump were seriously injured. Curfew was imposed. Most of the people from the village fled to nearby jungle fearing arrest and for fear of police violence.

Even a regional movement, thanks to ABVP, a BJP student wing of Osmania University. Like the Telangana movement got communalised when six Muslims of Adilabad district were burnt alive on 8th July in a village which is located on the border of Maharashtra and Andhra Pradesh. Miscreants set fire to a minority house in Watoli village, Adilabad district. Nearby Bhainsa town has a communal history and hence government is quite alert. Among those killed in Watile village are Mehboob Khan, Noman, Arsalan, Rizwan, Safiyah Begum and two year old toddler Tuba Mahosh.

On 12th July Agra's Mantola region saw eruption of communal violence. A truck carrying a sick goat for cure to hospital brushed against some people of the other community and argument began between the two groups belonging to different religions and soon stones flew and properties, shops, houses and vehicles began to be burnt and firing also took place. The police also had to fire. The DIG on duty escaped by a hair's breadth in the private firing. People were firing from the roofs of their houses. The Police force had to be increased in the area including PAC. The rioting was controlled with great difficulty.

Moradabad came under bout of communal violence again on 8th August when a procession of Kavadyas (Shiv Bhagats carrying Gangese water) was not allowed to be taken out from a Muslim Mohallah passing through a mosque. First the Kavadyas were confronted with the police and then they began firing on the mosque. Since Iftar time was nearing police was not ready to take any risk and Kavadyas were insisting on passing through the Muslim Mohallah.

When Muslims came out for Tarawih prayers Kavadyas tried to stop them and then they went berserk and began setting fire to motorcycles and other vehicles and they also set fire to police vehicles. They also stoned a mosque nearby. They also set fire to many trucks parked nearby. Also from below the bridge firing took place which happens to be a majority populated area. This shows it was well planned measure.

On 22 August in Jabalpur a town in M.P. two communities on the question of a religious procession and in no time stoning began and police had to clamp curfew in 6 police thana areas. In these clashes 1 person were injured, some quite seriously. Jabalpur also has communal history. It had witnessed first major communal violence of independent India in 1961.

On 25th August Bahraich in U.P. witnessed outbreak of violence. Bahraich is also highly communally sensitive area. Some dispute arose between groups of two communities outside a mosque and soon it assumed violent form and both the groups started pelting stones at each other and some even resorted to firing in which one person who was seriously injured died while being taken to hospital in Lucknow. Several persons were injured in rioting.

On 25th August communal violence broke out in Titwala, in Thane district on the occasion of Janmashtami. Some Hindu miscreants attacked Muslim youth and started beating them and damaged several properties and vehicles belonging to Muslims. A Muslim delegation with pictures of violence met home minister of Maharashtra Shri R.R.Patil. These miscreants are roaming around in Muslim Mohallahs and Muslims of the area are living in fear of being attacked. The police role, the delegation alleged, was also questionable.

On 2nd September on the day of Eid communal violence erupted in Newasa in Ahmadnagar district of Maharahtra. The police, it is alleged, played highly partisan role and those Muslims who went to police station to file FIR were themselves arrested under 307 and sent to jail. This happens very often and so Muslims generally avoid even filing FIRs. Many Muslims fled Nawasa and took refuge in Ahmednagar city. In this riot in Nawasa, Muslims were attacked with knives and swords and one Zaki's office was totally ransacked and yet police took no action. On the contrary action was taken by the police against Muslims and several of them arrested under section 307.

On 3rd September riot broke out in Ujjain, M.P. which has large Muslim population. In this riot two persons were killed and 16 injured It is said that riot broke out in Daulatganj area of old city when a shopkeeper installed Ganesh idol in his shop adjacent to a mosque. But it is not clear whether rioting broke out only for installation of idol or something happened around it. Apparently installing idol in a shop, even near a mosque, should not be cause enough for communal violence.

On 7th September communal violence broke out in Aduni Tehsil of Kurnool district in Andhra Pradesh in which hundreds of people were injured of which three injured people were quite serious. The cause was what happens often-music before mosque. Police had to resort to baton charge repeatedly to disperse the mob. Mob on both sides was resorting to stone pelting. This stone pelting went on for more than 4 hours and then police had to resort to firing in air. Ganesh idols were being taken for immersion in nearby Canal. This procession stopped near a mosque and went on playing music and the whole trouble erupted. Both the groups had brought stones in autos and trucks.

Next violence broke out in Nandurbar, a tribal area in Maharashtra on 8th September. This also happened when Ganesh idols were being taken for immersion Two persons were killed and several were injured. The violence broke out mainly because of illegal Ganpati Mandal and Muslims allege that Inspector Ramesh Patil was mainly responsible for this violence and he played very partisan role and terrorised Muslims. Here too those Muslims whose properties were destroyed and who went to lodge FIR were arrested under section 353,32 Muslims were arrested whereas only 12 non-Muslims were arrested. And under section 302, 6 Muslims were arrested and under section 307, 12 Muslims were arrested. The Muslims of Nandurbar were so terrorised that those who had lived for years they are not prepared to go back to their houses.

On 14th September the biggest riot of the year took place in Gopalgarh, Bharatpur Rajasthan in which 11 persons were killed and nine of them by one sided police firing inside mosque. Bharatpur mainly Meo Muslims live. There was disputed land of cemetery which Hindus claimed that it was a pond of water for their cattle which Panchayat has wrongly allotted for cemetery to Muslims.

Ashok Gehlot has miserably failed in controlling communal situation in his state. In 2010 also Rajasthan witnessed two big riots in Saroda and Mangal Thana and in both these places police openly played partisan role. In Saroda, Udaipur district 30 Muslim houses were burnt in presence of District Magistrate and SP which was very serious offence on the part of high government officials and Gehlot did not even suspend them. I personally urged upon him to suspend these officials and large number of Muslims gave Dharna outside his office but he took no action. With a result that communal minded police officials became very bold and other sensitive places too serious communal riots occurred.

When riots took place in Gopalgarh initially Gehlot dismissed it as mere land dispute but Mrs. Sonia Gandhi rebuked him and he suspended Collector and SP Communal situation in Rajasthan is very bad and Gehlot has mishandled it. BJP is openly using communal card to come back to power and Gehlot does nothing. Even the Congress delegation and M.Ps delegation felt Muslims were killed by one sided police firing. Muslims of Rajasthan are very angry with the CM Mr. Gehlot and many of them even boycotted his official functions.

Though Bharatpur as such is a communally sensitive district, Gopalgarh, a village in that district, had never known communal violence and Hindus and Muslims had lived in peace and harmony. Meo Muslims are even otherwise culturally half Hindus and many have Hindu names and observe all Hindu festivals. BJP often complains that Muslims are not part of mainstream and that is why communal prejudices remain alive. Though in a democracy rights do not accrue and right to live cannot be conditional, in Bharatpur Muslims are very much Hinduised, even if it is a condition. And yet we see such horrible communal violence.

Another riot took place in Rudrapur, Uttarakhand, a BJP ruled state. Rudrapur too had no communal history but it saw serious communal rioting. It seems in Rudrapur a deliberate attempt was made to incite communal violence. There was no spontaneous incident leading to communal violence. No one could be identified. Two attempts were made, one failed and one succeeded in inciting violence.

In first incident someone kept pages of Qur'an tied in a red cloth as if dipped in blood near a Sani temple on 28th September night. When worshippers came on the morning of 29th September they found it. It appeared as if the cloth was dipped in blood. Both Hindus and Muslims were angry but the police controlled the situation arguing with Muslims that Hindus too are angry.

But second attempt succeeded when on 2nd October, Gandhi Jayanti some pages on which Arabic letters were written tied in a green polythyne bag. The bits of paper were mixed with some kind of meat and the bag was kept near the same temple. First a crowd of 150 Muslims gathered first around 6-30 in the morning and then the crowd grew up to 800 and became violent. In this violent eruption some 38 policemen and district officials were injured. Then the Hindu mob came from the other side and now situation went totally out of control.

According to the police more than 30 civilians were injured and some 100 vehicles were torched. The Delhi-Nainital Highway was full of burnt vehicles near Rudrapur and mere steel skeletons were left. More than 100 shops were totally looted and destroyed. The FIR names in all 37 persons of whom 24 have been arrested. The situation would have been saved if the district administration and police had acted promptly on 29th September itself and arrested the miscreants. The state government therefore, replaced DM and IG police to restore peace.

This was the account of communal riots which took place during 2011 and it would be seen that all these riots took place on extremely petty issues. It can be seen that eruption of communal violence on such petty issues is possible only because due to constant communal propaganda strong prejudices prevail and there is total lack of confidence in each other. Also the police is prejudiced against Muslims and often sides with miscreants aggravating violence and thirdly poverty and unemployment makes it possible for large crowds to gather and take part in rioting.

Unless these factors are addressed it would be very difficult to ensure total communal peace in our country.

Index